CAPTIVATE

PRESENTATIONS THAT
ENGAGE AND
INSPIRE

CAPTIVATE

PRESENTATIONS THAT ENGAGE AND INSPIRE

STEVE HUGHES

WATERFIELD PRESS
ST. LOUIS

Requests for permission to reproduce any part of this work should be mailed to the publisher at:

Waterfield Press
1001 Alsace Court
St. Louis, MO 63017
WaterfieldPress.com

This publication is designed to provide accurate and authoritative information in regard to the subject matter covered. It is sold with the understanding that the publisher is not engaged in rendering legal, accounting, or other professional service. If legal advice or other expert assistance is required, the services of a competent professional person should be sought.

Hughes, Stephen R.
Captivate: presentations that engage and inspire/Steve Hughes.
First edition

ISBN-13: 978-0615464725
ISBN-10: 0615464726

1. Business Communication.   2. Public Speaking.   3. Presentation Skills.

Cover design by Daniel Barrozo, the Ink Studio
Author photo by Allison Light, Flash Creative Photography

Printed in the United States of America

10 9 8 7 6 5 4 3 2 1

To Mary Anne, Cali, and Bizzy—
the three most important women in my life.

Contents

Afterword   209

Acknowledgments   211

Appendices

Notes   225

Index   229

About the Author   237

PRELUDE

1

"They Can't Make Me Speak": The Memphis Story

Each time we face our fear, we gain strength, courage, and confidence in the doing.

—Anonymous

I'll never forget October 3, 1991—the night that changed my life. I was in my first year of business school when I got a phone call from my friend, Lynn, asking me for a "favor." The two of us volunteered for a worldwide non-profit based in San Antonio, Texas, and from time-to-time the organization called on certain volunteers to give presentations to its members. This was one of those times. Here's how the conversation unfolded.

"Steve, we would love for you to help us out by giving a talk to the St. Louis chapter in about four weeks. Are you up for it?" Lynn asked.

"Sure!" I said. (I've always been eager-to-please. But I wasn't fully aware of what I was getting myself into.)

"Great. Here are the details: It'll be on Monday night, November 4th at 7:00 pm. You'll speak for about 45 minutes and we expect the audience to be about 450 people. So we—"

"Wait a second. I thought I heard you say 450 people." I gulped.

"Yes, 450 people."

"Heh, heh." A brief, uncomfortable chuckle escaped my lips. "Wow. That's quite a large audience. What am I supposed to talk about?" I asked, not sure I really wanted to hear the answer.

Lynn gave me the details, suggested a few resources, and ended with, "Don't worry, you'll do great. Thanks."

Click.

I'm not sure how long it took me to hang up the phone. The time-space continuum seemed to collapse upon itself. It was somewhere between 10 seconds and a fortnight.

Like many people who are asked to address a large crowd for the first time, I found my mind torn between two competing thoughts: Speculative optimism that I could succeed at the task and sheer terror accompanied by a mental image of me curled up next to the podium in the fetal position.

Recognizing that others were counting on me, and goaded on by sheer pride, I kept going. I decided to make this talk as good as humanly possible. I read as much material as I could find. I studied what other speakers had said in similar situations, and I sought advice from people who had spoken in front of large groups. I tried to muster plenty of confidence, but a nagging voice remained in the back of my mind that said it was all too much. That I didn't belong up there behind the microphone. That I was going to be so bad that even my mom would be ashamed. Who was I fooling?

As the day crept closer, I entertained secret hopes that the meeting would get cancelled or postponed, or that everyone attending would suddenly lose their sense of direction and never arrive. Since neither scenario was likely to come to fruition, I had to keep preparing.

Two days before the presentation, I was so distraught that I skipped a day and a half of classes and devoted my full attention to the talk. And then it struck me: *I could just skip town and drive to Memphis.*

Why Memphis? It was the first city to pop into my mind. It's about three hours from St. Louis. Plus, it has great barbeque. I figured if I wasn't physically in town, no one could make me speak. This is no joke. The thought of talking to 450 people for nearly an hour was an unmitigated freak-out. I seriously contemplated The Memphis Plan because I had to have an escape route.

Finally, the day arrived. I had done everything I could think of to get ready, yet I was still a mess. I had no appetite. I couldn't concentrate. And as I drove to the meeting along Highway 64, I passed a sign that read "Highway 270 South— Memphis—Next Exit." I have to admit that making that left turn was awfully tempting.

I never drove to Memphis.

I delivered the speech, the crowd was kind, and even though I can't remember a word I said, I know this: I didn't die.

And despite the fact that the entire experience was utterly nerve-wracking, I have to admit, when all was said and done, I felt curiously energized by the whole thing.

Ironically, after business school I ended up taking a job in advertising that required almost daily presentations to clients (many times with millions of dollars on the line). I soon realized that I had to become a better speaker— fast.

In order to do so, I made it a point to observe men and women giving presentations to see what worked and what didn't. I was fascinated by the subtle and not-so-subtle things presenters did to bring their material to life, to engage audiences, and to change minds.

Two interesting things resulted from this "research." First, my overarching fear of public speaking was transformed into a passion. Second, I discovered that anyone (and I mean anyone) can become a really good presenter.

Great, Steve, but What Does This Mean for Me?

If you're fearful like I was, you're in good company. Public speaking has been at or near the top of the list of things Americans fear most since researchers first began tracking such things in the 1970s. (It even beats out dying, heights,...and zombies.)[1]

The good news is that you can overcome this fear and improve your skills at the same time. Outstanding presenters are not blessed with a special gene that makes them shine in front of an audience. They just do a bunch of little things well. And so can you.

Plus, good speaking skills are not just a "nice to have" asset, they're essential. According to *Harvard Business Review*[2], a leader's most important asset is the ability to communicate ideas effectively, whether one-on-one, to 10 people in a conference room, or to an audience of hundreds.

So to help you on both fronts, I give you this book: *Captivate*. Merriam-Webster[3] defines the word "captivate" to mean "to attract and hold the attention of (someone) by being interesting" and "to influence and dominate...with an irresistible appeal"—two things every speaker wants to do. And, if you think about it, every time you make a presentation, your audience is quietly saying, "Wow me. Make this interesting." They want to be enthralled by your information, your insights, your slides, and your delivery. They want an engaging experience that will enrich their work and/or personal lives. Helping you to be that speaker is what this book is all about.

2

How to Use This Book

Do or do not. There is no try.
—Yoda, Jedi Master

The concept behind *Captivate* is to provide you, the busy professional, with quick solutions to your most burning public speaking challenges. These solutions are not only based on the latest research, but have also been field-tested and proven effective.

Since there are approximately one million books (give or take) on presentation skills, here's what makes *Captivate* unique:

- The book's layout follows the recommended sequence for putting a presentation together from the ground up. Reading it sequentially will give you the most comprehensive plan for developing and delivering, world-class presentations.

- At the same time, special care has been taken to carefully label and construct each chapter such that it stands on its own and can be read in a short amount of time. This means that you can also use this book as a handy reference guide to quickly review just the information you need, right when you need it.

- Each chapter ends with a **"FAST APP"** designed to help you apply what you've just learned right away.

- And hopefully, you'll find this book quite readable—maybe even fun. It contains real-world anecdotes, stories, illustrations, and tips designed to drive home points and illuminate your learning. No, presentation skills development doesn't have to be boring.

Captivate is laid out as follows:

- **Part One—Crafting Your Talk** (Chapters 3–9), spells out how to assemble your presentation for maximum impact.

- **Part Two—Making It Engaging** (Chapters 10–16), offers ideas and strategies to invigorate your material with crowd-pleasing examples and illustrations.

- **Part Three—Delivering Your Speech** (Chapters 17–22), gives you proven and easy-to-follow physical techniques for commanding the room.

- **Part Four—Polishing Your Skills** (Chapters 23–27), covers the final details you need to sharpen your delivery, be prepared for the unexpected, manage your nerves, and build on your successes.

- **The Appendices** at the end of the book contain helpful templates, links, and other resources to further your development.

One More Thing

To keep things fresh and avoid endless redundancies, I've used the following words interchangeably:

- Presentation, speech, talk, lecture

- Audience, listeners, group, attendees, participants, crowd

To be sure, each of these words has its own nuanced definition, but I think you'll agree that variety trumps boring.

If you're ready to accelerate your career, look smart when you talk, and captivate audiences every time you speak, then keep reading.

And remember, if all goes wrong, there's always Memphis.*

* If this reference doesn't make sense, read "They Can't Make Me Speak" in Chapter 1.

PART ONE:
CRAFTING YOUR TALK

3

The Take-Home Message

The odds of hitting your target go up dramatically
when you aim at it.

—Anonymous

It's the first day of your long-awaited summer vacation. You and your friends pile into the car and start driving. No destination. No plan. You just hop onto the nearest interstate and motor away.

As freewheeling and fun as this may sound, does it sound like the recipe for a successful and satisfying trip? Probably not. How will you know when you arrive if you don't have a specific destination in mind? Do you have the clothes, gear, and essentials that you need? Iffy at best. When you start out this way, your chances of having a great vacation are "slim to none" (which, incidentally, was the name of my band in college).

Whether you revel in or scoff at the prospect of a destinationless vacation, think about the last time you sat in an audience listening to someone else's presentation. Did it have a clear destination—i.e., a singular message? Did you walk away knowing exactly what you were supposed to do, why you were supposed to do it, and when it needed to happen?

All too often, speakers are so focused on getting a speech

written and delivered that they don't step back to evaluate whether their audience will grasp the heart of what they have to say. They assume their main point—in and among their data, examples, and conclusions—is perfectly obvious.

News flash: It isn't. Covering all the information doesn't guarantee that your audience will understand what they're supposed to do with it.

Returning to the vacation example: The first step in taking a holiday is choosing a destination. Only then can you decide how to get there—via car, plane, or rickshaw. Let alone decide which kind of shoes to pack.

The Take-Home Message

Just as determining your destination is the first step in planning a vacation, the first task in crafting a great speech is figuring out its purpose, otherwise called the *Take-Home Message*. Your Take-Home Message is the key idea, recommendation, or instruction you want uppermost in your audience's mind when you finish speaking. After you develop this, you can design a speech to land your message right in their laps.

The Two Questions Approach

A quick way to zero in on your Take-Home Message is to ask yourself these two questions:

First: "*What* do I want my audience to do, think, or feel?"
Approve funding? Hire additional people? View the competition differently? Consider a new product offering?

Second: "*Why* do I want them to do, think, or feel this?"
Obviously, because it will mean you've won them over to your point of view, which may mean a sale, support for a project, or future gigs for you. But what about your audience? Answering the "why" question from the audience's point of view gives your presentation traction. So get personal. What's in it for *them*? Will they save time or money? Get more autonomy or recognition? Basically, why should they care?

Write It Out

Once you have a clear Take-Home Message, go ahead and write it at the top of your presentation notes and use it as a roadmap, so to speak. Then, as you write each portion of your presentation, ask yourself, "Does this reinforce my Take-Home Message?" If so, great. If not, consider revising the section or leaving it out altogether.

Even when you have very complex information to deliver, your audience still needs a relatively simple and easy-to-understand message they can embrace and walk away with. Let your Take-Home Message guide you throughout the writing process.

Take-Home Message Examples

Here are some examples of Take-Home Messages from actual presentations:

- *I want our organization to increase our employee retention rate by 5% so that we can reduce our recruiting and training costs.*

- *I'd like you to retain us as your firm of record because our unique expertise will help your company save money and increase your market share at the same time.*

- *When you recognize the five decision-making styles people use in business, you will be more successful and get higher acceptance when presenting new ideas.*

- *This policy change will require more work on your part, but it will allow you to have more contact and time with customers.*

Each one of these THMs has a clear action and an equally clear benefit for the audience.

Save Prep Time

Of all the fabulous suggestions in this book, determining your Take-Home Message is the one that will reduce your preparation time the most.

A brand manager who attended one of my seminars used to spend five to six hours preparing quarterly presentations to present to her company's regional directors. Her biggest problem, she said, was deciding what to include and what to leave out (not to mention that she wrote her presentation in PowerPoint® instead of Word®—a big no-no). When she spent just five minutes crafting her Take-Home Message first, she cut her preparation time by a third. It made it much easier to zero in on what mattered and what didn't.

You'll see similar savings in time and effort if you identify a strong Take-Home Message before you start writing. It's kind of like deciding where you want to go on vacation before you get behind the wheel.

FAST APP

What is the single most important point in your presentation—i.e., the one you want your audience to walk away with?

Write it down in one crisp sentence and be sure to include the "why."

You'll be off to a flying start.

PowerPoint and Microsoft Word are registered trademarks of Microsoft Corporation.

4

Put Yourself in Their Shoes

For some players you simply tell them the play and they
immediately know it; others must be shown diagrams
before they can form their own mental image of what to do;
and still others won't really grasp the play until
they physically run through it on the field
*so that they can **feel** the play, as well as **see** and **hear** it.*
—John Madden, Super Bowl-winning
coach of the Oakland Raiders

Suppose you were asked to give a speech on the Civil War. (The Civil War? Just work with me here.) How would the speech differ if the audience were a small group of history professors as opposed to an auditorium full of seventh graders? What if the speaking venue were in the Deep South versus in Boston? Or, first thing in the morning versus in the late afternoon? You get the idea.

The subject matter remains the same, but how you serve up the information can change dramatically depending on the audience, as well as influencing factors like setting and time of day. The better job you do of putting yourself in the audience's shoes and seeing the world from their perspective, the better your material will resonate.

The same holds true for business presentations. The most

successful business presenters have their finger on the pulse of their audience even before they draft their speech. They know what makes their listeners tick; what they consider important, how they think, what concerns them, and how they make decisions. The best way to start gathering this information is to ask classic probing questions.

Six Points of Audience Analysis

Let's ask six classic questions to unpack the six major audience aspects that will influence your speech:

1. **WHO?**

   Who will be sitting in the seats? Are they under thirty, in their fifties, or a mix of ages? Mostly male, mostly female, or 50/50? Senior management or junior staffers?

   How familiar are they with your subject matter? Do they work with it on a daily basis or do you need to give them a little context before you launch into the meat (or tofu) of your talk? Are they your coworkers and colleagues, or are you an outside speaker? What's their educational background? Is attendance optional or mandatory?

2. **WHAT?**

   What is going on in your audience's world that may affect how they receive your message? Is their company coming off its best year ever? Have there been recent layoffs or a salary freeze? What past experience do they have with you, your department, or your organization? What stories might they be telling themselves about you and your topic? Remember, your presentation is just one slice of one day in the lives of these busy professionals. How can you break through the noise of their day-to-day tasks and be heard?

3. WHEN?

At what time of day is the presentation taking place? In the morning when most people are relatively fresh and focused? Right after lunch when people are fighting off postprandial somnolence, a.k.a. a food coma? At the end of the day when they're tired and eager to go home?

4. WHERE?

Where is the presentation taking place? If it's not on their home turf, understand that your audience will be less at ease. This applies to people outside your organization as well as folks in interdepartmental meetings.

If the speech is taking place on their turf, your audience will be more comfortable, but also more likely to take a call or permit interruptions during the presentation.

5. WHY?

Out of the seven billion plus people on the planet, why has this particular group been singled out to listen to your presentation? And why are they hearing it at this moment in time?

6. HOW?

How does your audience like to receive information? While it may be fairly homogeneous in other ways, the crowd will almost certainly be made up of different kinds of learners.

Here's a quick overview of the three primary adult learning styles: [1]

Auditory learners (20 to 30% of the population) learn best through what they hear. As you might imagine, they are big fans of books on tape and probably have 6,000 songs in their iTunes® library. Auditory learners are not as interested in looking at your PowerPoint slides and flip charts, or even looking at you, because they're taking it all in through their ears. They may even cock their head to one side to hear you more clearly.

Visual learners (30 to 40% of the population) are primarily engaged by seeing things. Visual learners prefer graphic representations of your key points—pictures, graphs, and charts—whereas *print learners*, a subset of visual learners, respond well to text in PowerPoint presentations and handouts. These visual types have to "see it to believe it."

Kinesthetic learners (30 to 50% of the population) prefer to process information by physically interacting with the material—handling a prototype, flipping through a handout, taking notes, asking and answering questions, even watching you move about the room.

A perfect presentation engages all three learning styles so that no one is left out. To be clear, you don't have to address all three types at every moment. Rather, be sure to actively include material designed for each style at some point(s) during your presentation.

Think about your last speech. Were any learning styles of your audience overlooked? What changes could you make in your next presentation to include all three types?

Putting Your Audience Analysis to Work

So, how does gathering all this data about the audience make you a better communicator? The more your presentation is customized to their needs, the better you'll resonate with and persuade them. Customizing includes everything from word choice (e.g., never refer to a law firm as a "company") to level of detail (the higher up the chain of command you go, the more they'll want the big picture and less detail).

Here are a few examples:

- An admissions officer at a top-20 business school received high marks on her 25-minute "About Our School" message by encouraging students to text their questions to her throughout the presentation. She then answered these questions in real time. The Millennials in her audience, accustomed to social media and user-generated-content, welcomed the chance to have a voice during her talk, as opposed to being silent observers. Plus, they appreciated the anonymity of texting vs. raising their hands and calling attention to themselves in front of strangers.

- A consultant to financial services companies invested extra time and resources to upgrade his research material in order to gain more credibility with his audiences. He noticed that his audience responded better to a higher caliber of research. In addition, they asked more insightful questions and gave him less pushback than in previous presentations.

- Personally, I revamped the order of my full-day *"Captivate"* workshop such that the majority of the active, stand-up presentations and exercises take place in the afternoon, when people's attention tends to drag. I've noticed a big difference in engagement and retention.

It's simple: Know your audience. → Tailor your speech to them. → Get better results.

Three Quick Audience Research Ideas

What do you do when you don't know much about the audience you're presenting to? Here are three ideas you can explore before crafting your speech:

Idea One: *Ask them.*
Contact the person who asked you to speak or the head of the department you'll be addressing. You may not be able to talk to the company president or the key decision maker, but you may gain valuable insights from an administrative assistant or other employees. How about talking to vendors, partners, distributors, or current or former customers? Several five-minute phone interviews or email exchanges can yield a wealth of information, and most people are more than happy to help.

Idea Two: *Make use of that obscure little search engine called Google®.* (You may have heard of it.)
Go beyond just a basic company search. Find discussion boards, blogs, and other waters where your audience swims online. A world of information is at your fingertips, waiting to be discovered.

Idea Three: *Tap into your network* (through LinkedIn®, Twitter®, or the like.)

(But be careful. Among the insights into how your audience members see the world, you may come across a few questionable Spring Break photos.)

FAST APP

Make a quick list of everything you know about the audience for your next speech. Answer the questions: Who? What? When? Where? Why? and How?

Determine what you still need to know. Then, devise a creative plan to get your hands on that info.

You can use the Know Your Audience *Worksheet in* Appendix B. *For a free downloadable* Know Your Audience Worksheet, *visit* www.HitYourStride.com.

---

iTunes is a registered trademark of Apple Inc.

Google is a registered trademark of Google Inc.

LinkedIn is a registered trademark of LinkedIn Corporation.

Twitter is a registered trademark of Twitter, Inc.

5

Stick the Landing:
The Call-to-Action

Just do it.

—Nike tagline
(the best Call-to-Action ever)

Every commercial on TV or ad on the Internet starts out as a few paragraphs of concise text on an 8 1/2" x 11" sheet of paper. This document, called a creative brief, spells out everything the advertiser and their agency need to consider while crafting the commercial—including the most important element: the Call-to-Action, or CTA.

The CTA is a sentence or phrase the advertiser wants you, the viewer, to remember after seeing the commercial.

Many CTAs are specific and retail-oriented:

- "Drive away in a new Jetta for only $329 a month." [Volkswagen]
- "15 minutes could save you 15% or more on car insurance." [GEICO]
- "Hurry, our Sell-A-Thon ends Saturday." [Toyota]

Others—often brand-oriented—are attitudinal:

- "Just do it." [Nike]
- "Always low prices. Always." [Walmart]

- "I'm lovin' it." [McDonald's]

Either way, the commercial ends with the CTA—or what *New York Times* best-selling author Roy H. Williams calls "the lasting mental image."[1] Every speech you make should conclude the same way.

Instead, how do <u>most</u> business presentations end? With a lame Q&A session. Wamp, wamp. Question & Answer sessions are valuable, but too many factors are out of the presenter's control during that time. The conversation can veer off topic, the mood of the room can turn negative, people may ask questions pertaining only to them, or the audience may simply get bored.

The remedy is to bring the Q&A session to a close and *then* leave your audience with a single task, recommendation, vision, or thought, summed up in a clear statement: your CTA. Just like a top gymnast earns higher scores by sticking the landing on a dismount, you'll get better results from your talk if you end with a strong CTA.

Crafting a CTA

How do you craft a good CTA? Simply reword your Take-Home Message (see Chapter 3) into action-oriented terms. For example, here are the Take-Home Message and CTA for a speech on Internet security for local business owners:

Take-Home Message:
Business owners should set up tighter security protocols because it is too easy for former employees to gain access to the company's computer system and steal information.

CTA:
Protect your online assets and prevent unnecessary legal action by setting up online security guidelines for your company in the next 30 days.

Most of the time I write my CTA right after I finalize my Take-Home Message. Some people prefer to identify their Take-Home Message, then craft their speech, and finally compose a CTA after determining the speech's content. Your call.

A CTA for Every Speech?

You may be thinking: "Steve, this is all well and good, but often I'm just updating my department on a project. They're not supposed to do anything afterward, so I don't need a CTA, right?"

Actually, a CTA is still a good idea. Even if you are not making a recommendation or trying to convince your audience to change their thinking or behavior, you still want them to walk away with a clear message. For an update on a project, the CTA could be: "We're running two weeks behind our original schedule, but we can get back on track if we repurpose three additional people to this project immediately."

Again, consider the way a TV commercial showcases the product and brand name, and then ends with a statement designed to inspire action. Every viewer, whether the product interests them or not, gets the message. You want the same response in the minds of your listeners.

But Wait. There's More...

A strong, clear CTA has a secondary benefit. When it's the last thing your audience hears, they will give it more import and it will be more memorable. This is thanks to the phenomenon psychologists refer to as the "recency effect." The recency effect states that people will tend to place extra weight on the last thing they hear. This is why, when presented with a list of items to remember, people tend to recall them in reverse order. In other words, they start with the last thing they hear (the most recent) and work backwards. So, why not capitalize on the recency effect and leave your audience with a tight CTA they'll more readily recall later?

Just do it.

FAST APP

The next time you're watching your favorite TV show, instead of zapping past the commercials, study a few of them. Pay close attention to the last five seconds of each spot. Identify the Call-to-Action. Is it specific? Does it create a sense of urgency? If someone were to ask you, could you say without hesitation what the commercial wants you to do, think, or feel?

If you're not a TV watcher, look for the Call-to-Action in other forms of advertising, like radio commercials or unavoidable short ads that precede videos online.

6

A Confused Mind Always Says "No"

*I used to tell my husband that, if he could make me
'understand' something, it would be clear to all
the other people in the country.*
—Eleanor Roosevelt,
First Lady, author, activist

You've written your Take-Home Message, analyzed
your audience, and established your Call-to-Action. Now is an
ideal time—before writing the body of your presentation—to
consider the power of clarity in a presentation. The best way to
illustrate the importance of clarity is with a jar of jelly.
Actually, a study of how people buy jelly.[1]

In the late 1990s, a couple of professors set out to show the
world the effects of clarity and choice on people's ability to
make decisions. They conducted a unique experiment at a
grocery store on the East Coast. Shoppers were presented with
displays of either 6 or 24 varieties of jams and jellies and the
researchers then recorded how much people bought. The people
who were shown the larger assortment, 24 jars, were initially
more intrigued by the display, but when it came time to make a
purchase, the shoppers who were offered only 6 varieties were
10 times more likely to buy.

The professors' conclusion? Too many choices confused
the shoppers. As much as they might have initially thought they

liked having a greater number of choices, that greater number ultimately made it harder for them to decide which jelly was best. The choice wasn't clear. And when the human mind gets confused, it says, "No, thank you." (It really just says "no," but I think adding "thank you" is more polite. That's just how I roll.)

Similar research results were generated in a study[2] involving employees at 647 companies who were offered 401(k) plans ranging in size from 2 to 59 investment funds. More people participated in the 401(k) plans, and at the proper risk level, when they had fewer funds to choose from. Once again, less proved to be more.

What does this mean for you, the public speaker? It means your audience will more likely go along with what you're proposing as long as they don't get confused at any point during your speech.

"No duh," you might say. However, think about a presentation when the audience didn't accept your proposal, adopt your recommendation, or buy what you were selling. Could it be that important audience members, perhaps even the key decision makers, were bewildered at some point and took the safe route of simply saying, "No"?

Of course they could have said "no" for any one of a thousand reasons. But why not do everything within your power to present your listeners with a crystal clear message?

Common "Confusion Traps"

Here are some common causes of confusion in presentations:

Speaking Too Fast

Speaking in public naturally causes nervousness and an adrenaline rush. It's a holdover from earlier days when our fight-or-flight response to fearful situations meant the difference between life or death. As the adrenaline builds, we tend to speak faster. The trouble is, as speech gets faster, diction begins to fall off. Words slur and mix together. And audience comprehension plummets.

Covering Too Much Material in the Time Provided

A speaker may not talk too hurriedly, but if the speech is a rapid-fire information dump, the audience will be just as confused (and bored). People need time to process what they hear. Instead of flooding your audience with a non-stop fire hose full of data, offer them cool glasses of water at regular intervals throughout your talk. (See Chapter 19 for more on how to use the Pause.)

Using Insider Speak

Every industry has unique terms and phrases that are part of doing business. If you're speaking to an insider group, using some jargon is certainly okay. But if even one audience member is from another department or completely outside the industry, that person is at risk of being confused.

Using Unexplained Acronyms

Acronyms—wordy, clumsy titles or phrases reduced to cutesy alphabet-soup-like terms—are insider speak taken to a whole new level. Examples include: CFC, REIT, and SOA ("Solutions Oriented Architecture," voted the most confusing high-tech acronym of the decade 2000-2009 by the Global Language Monitor[3]). Some acronyms, like SUV and GDP, have become part of the vernacular. No big deal. But if you're not sure about using an acronym, remember: "If in doubt, spell it out."

Being Too Close to the Subject Matter
(The "Expert's Paradox")

Sometimes the speaker knows the ins and outs of the presentation's subject matter so deeply that he forgets how it sounds to someone else, especially a novice. He may assume, "This stuff is so obvious. How could anyone not know this?" Careful there, Smarty Pants, it may be new to a key audience member. The solution?

• Present your idea to a colleague or friend who is not familiar with your topic. If he understands it, chances are your audience will, too.

• Boil your message down to one sentence. Sort of like the way you did in writing your Take-Home Message.

• Summarize your speech in language that a seventh grader could understand. If it makes sense to a middle schooler, a CEO should be able to keep up.

Just as unforced errors in tennis can mean losing a match, inserting too much information or insider speak can prevent an otherwise strong presentation from carrying the day.

FAST APP

Do a quick scan of your next presentation. Put on an outsider's hat and notice any acronyms, jargon, or insider speak you may find yourself using. If you spot any, either add explanations or eliminate them.

7

SPARQ:
Grabbing Their Attention
from Word One

You never get a second chance to make a first impression.
—Head & Shoulders® shampoo commercial

How many times have you heard a speaker open with something like: "Good morning. It's great to be here. My name is John Doe. Today I'm going to talk about implementing a Six Sigma program in our Northeast Region..."? Or, "How is everybody doing today? I'd like to thank Janice Murphy for inviting me to speak. There are some really exciting things happening in the world of cost accounting..."? (Kill me now.)

Too often, speakers miss out on the brief, but *huge* opportunity at the beginning of their speech to get the audience engaged and eager to hear more. Even for topics that are considered boring. Banal opening statements like, "It's great to be here" communicate nothing of value. Worse still, they don't give the audience a reason to tune in. Why should they listen? What's keeping them from whipping out their smartphones? Heck, what's keeping them from faking a stomach virus and bolting for the door?

Your audience is constantly asking: "What's in it for me?" If you don't provide them with a good answer (and fast), then their attention, I'm sorry to say, has most likely left the building.

SPARQ

What you need to open with is a spark or, as I like to say, a "SPARQ." A SPARQ is a teaser, a quick burst of exciting content that grabs your audience's attention and whets their appetite for the rest of your speech. An effective SPARQ is unexpected, interesting, relevant, and quick.

(It may appear a bit ironic that I'm using an acronym right after I just railed against them in the previous chapter. Let me explain. It's certainly permissible to use acronyms as long as you clearly describe what they stand for, as I'm about to do. Problems arise when you casually toss around acronyms that your audience doesn't understand, without any explanation.)

SPARQ stands for: **S**urprising **S**tatistic, **P**icture, **A**necdote, **R**eal-life example, **Q**uestion, and **Q**uote. (Okay, those are actually two "Q"s, but SPARQ reads better and is more memorable with just one. Thanks for allowing me that bit of literary license.)

Let's look at these one by one:

S = Surprising Statistic

The right number(s) can be a powerful attention grabber. Opening a presentation by writing out a few key numbers on a flip chart piques the audience's curiosity as they wonder what one has to do with the other.

For example, a presenter selling an expensive product that offers big savings down the road might write the following on a flip chart:

2,000,000
10
54,000

Then he might say, "You're probably wondering what these numbers represent." After a brief pause, he can explain: "Two million represents the dollars you'll save in operating costs over the next 10 years, IF you're willing to spend an additional $54,000 for our system this year. Yes, our product involves a higher short-term investment, but today, let's cast a long-term vision." At the very least, this SPARQ reframes the issue in favorable terms for the speaker.

P = Picture (or short video)

We live in a visually oriented, media-driven society, so why not start your next presentation with an intriguing picture or video?

A COO at a mid-sized IT company used a picture to address a looming, yet overlooked problem within her organization. She got her listeners' attention by flashing an image of a huge iceberg floating in deep blue Arctic waters and saying, "For the past three quarters we have done a great job documenting our materials costs. However, these costs we've been tracking so carefully are only a small percentage of our total costs, just as only 10-20% of this iceberg is visible above the surface. A much bigger problem is our soaring vendor costs, which are a far greater predictor of profits, yet until now have gone largely unnoticed 'under the waterline.'" The audience was then open and curious to hear what she was going to say next and she was able to use the iceberg imagery throughout her talk by referring to seen and unseen costs above and below the surface.

A = Anecdote (or Story)

Human beings love anecdotes and stories. They are memorable and they get retold. They also allow us to deliver difficult truths in a more palatable way.

Let's say you need to address an audience made up of two factions who don't get along, like management and labor, or sales and marketing, or IT and…well…anybody. (Just kidding.) Your SPARQ could be: "We all know there's been some bad blood between the two groups here, but the problems we're facing can only be solved if we all work together. As I think about our situation, I'm reminded of a story about a veterinarian and a taxidermist in Ohio who decided to share some office space. They put a sign in their storefront window to advertise their offerings. It read: 'Come to us. Either way, you get your dog back.' [Pause for laughter.] If a veterinarian and a taxidermist, who work essentially at cross purposes, can find a way to work together, so can we. . . ."

By the way, that's an example of a three-sentence story. People think telling a story requires a chunk of time, but one of these mini stories can illustrate a point in less than 30 seconds. (For more info on how to tell a good story, see Chapter 12.)

R = Real-Life Example

You can also ignite interest with a really good analogy, metaphor, or illustration.

A media analyst at a Fortune 500 company once had

the unenviable task of asking senior management for $300,000 to purchase a new software program for her department. She chose an analogy that her listeners didn't see coming. She began her speech by saying, "Imagine you're shopping in your local grocery store. You walk up and down the aisles filling your cart to the brim with all the things you like. When you get to the cashier, she tells you that for every dollar you hand her, she will give you two dollars back *and* you get to keep your groceries. Not a bad deal, eh? Well, we've crunched the numbers on the new TR1000 software system, and you will see that for every dollar we invest in the program today, we will get two dollars back in savings inside of 48 months. Plus, we'll have more accurate and efficient media forecasts along the way." The analogy took only 15 seconds to relate, but it was just enough to pry open more than a few skeptical minds. (Yes, she got the funding.)

Q = Question

Asking a question (rhetorical or otherwise) at the outset of your presentation offers two benefits: It gets your audience thinking, and it communicates that you want them to be active participants.

An operations manager who wanted to highlight a new quarterly metric in his "state of the plant" meeting began his speech by asking, "What is the largest, single obstacle preventing us from achieving all of our Q4 goals?" He knew that there were plenty of ideas and opinions about the largest obstacle, but by asking a question he activated thinking and caused people to reflect.

If you want to figure out what question to ask, look over your presentation and find the one or two most challenging, interesting, or thought-provoking things you're going to say. Then turn one of them into a question and open with it.

Q = Quote

Another great speech opener is a good quotation. Nothing makes you look smarter faster than a well-stated quote from an historical figure, a business leader, a university professor, or even a personal friend. The quote doesn't have to be directly related your topic. It just needs to set up the point you're going to make.

For instance, a speech about upcoming changes in your accounting department doesn't require a hard-to-find, catchy quote about debits and credits. (Good luck finding one of those.) You simply need a quote that highlights the concept of improvement. For example, you could say, "Winston Churchill once said, 'There's nothing wrong with change, if it is in the right direction.'" After that you're ready to launch into the proposed changes.

Coming up with a SPARQ for your presentation doesn't require vast creative abilities or lots of time. All you need is a few minutes of thinking time. Determine what you need to communicate and then find the right SPARQ to fire up your audience's attention.

Keep in mind, your SPARQ should be the absolute first thing you do in your presentation (i.e., prior to introducing yourself or anything else). Then, if the audience doesn't know who you are, briefly introduce yourself right after. Keep your self-intro short—just your name, title, company name, and maybe one nugget about why you're qualified to be speaking to them. Your entire introduction should be no longer than 10-15 seconds.

Note: SPARQs are not just for presentation openings. If your speech is 30 minutes or longer, consider using a SPARQ to introduce each main section of your talk. That way, you infuse your topic (no matter how boring it may seem) with interesting and tasty cerebral candy.

FAST APP

Think of the material you plan to cover in your next presentation. Is there a singular fact or insight that the audience won't expect? What statistic, picture, anecdote, real-life example, question, or quote would cause them to lean forward in their chairs and say, "Tell me more..."?

When in doubt, start with a question. It's the easiest SPARQ to execute. For more examples of good SPARQs, visit www.HitYourStride.com.

Head & Shoulders is a trademark of The Procter & Gamble Company.

8

The Universal Speech Outline

When you've only got two ducks, they're always in a row
—Rich Bowen, author and open source pioneer

I'm going to go out on a limb here and take a guess: I bet you're not a big fan of squandering precious daylight hours. If that's the case, I suggest you don't even think about giving your next presentation without developing an outline.

Outlining is quick, effective, and easy. Best of all, unlike a speech written out word-for-word, an outline provides you with a roadmap for your presentation without tying you down to a fixed route; that is, specific words.

You might be thinking, "I haven't done an outline since middle school. I'm not sure I still know how." Never fear. All the hard work has already been done for you...about 2,500 years ago in ancient Greece.

The Classic Speech Outline

The Greek philosophers like Aristotle, Plato, and company, didn't have cable, so they passed their time thinking about cool things like how to give a good speech and how to make a really good gyro.

For speeches, they settled on a pattern that goes something like this:

I. Introduction
Getting the audience's attention

II. Narrative
Delivering the message

III. Argument
Presenting evidence to back up the narrative

IV. Refutation
Anticipating and answering questions

V. Conclusion
Encouraging the audience to adopt the speaker's way of thinking

A 21st Century Take on the Classic

Here's a twenty-first-century take on that classic speech outline originally laid down by the fathers of rhetoric. To make it easier, I divide the outline into three distinct sections: The Beginning, The Middle, and The End. Ah, you may laugh. But don't let its simplicity fool you. When done correctly, this is a powerful way to be heard and understood.

THE BEGINNING
The beginning is a relatively brief part of your speech in which you have two very important goals: To get the

audience's attention and to let them know what you plan to cover.

Of course, you need to clearly connect the key message of your presentation to something that your audience cares about. So right out of the gate, you want to deliver your **SPARQ**, something creative and unexpected to get their attention (see Chapter 7 for more details).

Then, make a smooth transition to your **Take-Home Message**. Tell the audience what you want them to do, think, or feel and why (see Chapter 3).

Feel free to devote as much time as you need to frame the discussion and set up the body of your speech. Think of this section as the launching pad for the rest of your information.

THE MIDDLE

The middle is the main part of your presentation. Here you provide your key points or **rationale** to support your Take-Home Message.

How many points should you make? It's more art than science, but three main points seems to work well because it's enough to give your argument credibility and heft without overwhelming your audience. Of course, you're welcome to include more if the situation dictates. But keep in mind the psychological principle of overcompensating or "overselling"—going beyond what is needed to such a degree that your audience begins to question why you're pushing so hard.

No matter how many key points you use, always lead with your strongest material. Attention spans are short, and your time may get cut unexpectedly.

THE END

Now we come to the end of your presentation. I believe the biggest unreported crime in America today (besides the comb-over) is when speakers finish presentations poorly. Usually they say something like this: "Any questions?" Or, "That's my time. Thank you." *Wow. I'm inspired.*

A far superior conclusion (which is covered in depth in Chapter 5) is to end on a positive note by delivering your **Call-to-Action**—an action-oriented expression of the one thing you want your audience to do, think, or feel based on your presentation.

In order for your CTA to be the last thing your audience hears, you need to handle **Q&A** <u>before</u> you conclude. A lot of folks bristle, dare I say freak out, at the thought of not putting Q&A at the end of their presentation. Never fear. Just have your Q&A session as the second-to-last thing you do and follow it quickly with a strong CTA. (For more on how to confidently own the room during your Q&A session, check out the next chapter, Chapter 9.)

A Word about Evaluating Your Presentation

For eons, humans have asked this question: "How can I get an awesome body without eating well or working out?" You can't. Sadly, the same goes for improving your presentations. The only way to guarantee progress in your speaking abilities is to give speeches as often as possible and to take active steps to regularly evaluate your speaking performances. I suggest you assess the effectiveness of each presentation within the first 24 hours of giving it, while that material is fresh in your mind. At a minimum, a good self-evaluation identifies one thing you did well (that you want to continue), along with one thing you would like to improve upon for your next speech. (Check out Chapter 27 for more insight on conducting self-evaluations.)

True, your evaluation is not part of the speech itself. But I include it in the outline because it's *that* important to becoming a captivating speaker. A speech isn't complete until it's been evaluated.

The Universal Speech Outline

For all you visual learners, Figure 8.1 shows the layout of the *Universal Speech Outline*.

This outline works for any presentation, from a ten-minute project update to an hour-long speech or a full day of training. The only difference between a short presentation and a long one is the length of the middle, or rationale, section. This is understandably dictated by both the amount of material you have to support your primary message and the amount of time you've been given for your talk. When your time is short, it is essential to use your few strongest points. Of course, when you have more time, you'll be able to dig deeper, go further, and cover more ground.

Outlining versus Writing Out Your Presentation

The benefits and disadvantages of writing out a presentation word-for-word have been debated in public speaking circles as

BEGINNING	1. **SPARQ** Get their attention. 2. **Take-Home Message** Tell them why they're there, and give additional explanation to set up your topic and frame the discussion. (Introduce yourself, if needed.)
MIDDLE	3. **Rationale** Provide supporting facts and material to back up your Take-Home Message.
END	4. **Q&A** Answer any remaining questions from the audience and clear up any confusion about your topic. 5. **Call-to-Action** Send them off confidently to do, think, or feel what you want them to.
Self-Evaluation	6. Within 24 hours of your speech, identify **one thing you want to continue** to do and **one thing you'd like to improve** upon.

Figure 8. — Universal Speech Outline

hotly as Coke vs. Pepsi. Here's my take: Writing out your speech is valuable if it increases your confidence in the process. It can help you make sure you include everything you want to say, work out transitions, and get comfortable with the flow of the talk.

However, I am not in favor of memorizing a written-out speech like a script. Nor do I recommend speaking from a full-text document in front of an audience. The best presenters in the world deliver their material in a professional, yet conversational manner. Reading off a script and trying to get every last syllable perfect rarely comes across as natural. (And getting good at using a teleprompter takes a lot of hard work.)

Whether you write your speech word-for-word or simply jot down talking points, I suggest you use an outline, either as described in this chapter or with some other layout of your own choosing. Both when you practice and when you give the presentation, use the outline to jog your memory and keep yourself on track.

FAST APP

Write a bulleted outline for your next presentation before you start working on the finer details, and definitely before you structure any text slides or visuals in PowerPoint.

9

Mastering Q&A

You can tell whether a man is clever by his answers.
You can tell whether a man is wise by his questions.
—Naguib Mahfouz, winner of
the 1988 Nobel Prize in Literature

If speaking in public is regarded as America's top fear, then facing the Question & Answer session that concludes most presentations is a close second.

This fear is about as necessary as the first "r" in February. Still, people tend to hyperventilate at the prospect of fielding tough questions or, worse yet, not knowing the answer to one.

Why such consternation? Why the hand wringing? Because most people prepare for the presentation, but they fail to plan for the Q&A session. Gee, they don't prepare for Q&A and then they wonder why it doesn't go well. Hmmm.

In your case, let's put an end to that right now. As a captivating speaker, you can not only survive Q&A, you can also turn it into a powerful tool of influence. Of course, some presentations, like a keynote address, don't necessarily include Q&A, but 95% of business presentations do.

A good Q&A session goes way beyond a rehash of things already said. The goal of Q&A is not just to answer the audience's questions, but also to revisit parts of your speech in greater detail and cement the main points in your listeners' minds.

Seven Keys to Setting Up a Powerful Q&A

Here are seven quick, no-fail ways to set up a powerful Q&A session:

1. ***Plan ahead.***

   After you have crafted your presentation and practiced it at least once out loud (see Chapter 23), spend a few minutes thinking about the questions your audience is most likely to ask. Then, think about how you would answer these questions so you're ready when the moment arises.

   It may help to know that the most common questions asked in business presentations fall into one of five categories:

   a. **Financial** – How much will it cost? Where will the money come from? Will this be profitable? How can we shave costs?

   b. **Timing** – When will it happen? Why at that time? Why not sooner—or later?

   c. **Responsibility** – Who will do it? Does that person or team have the expertise to get it done? How will this affect me? My department? My team?

   d. **Feasibility** – How are we supposed to accomplish this? Do we have the required tools and resources? Is this goal realistic?

e. **Marketability** – Is there a market for this idea? Who would want to buy it, and why? How does our offering stack up against the competition's?

2. *Consider the weak points.*

Take an honest look at your presentation. Identify parts where your reasoning might be weak or the idea controversial. If anyone in your audience is going to take issue with what you say, they'll naturally start by attacking the soft underbelly of your assertions. First, see if there is anything you can do to strengthen these weaker parts. Then, put pen to paper (or finger to keyboard) and write out some ways you can address these concerns.

3. *Solicit a champion.*

Consider planting a question or two with a "friendly" member of the audience. Q&A sessions often take a little while to get going. Your champion can ask her question early on. As the audience relaxes into the session, they'll realize it's safe to ask questions and they'll become more vocal. Plus, it doesn't hurt to begin your Q&A with a question to which you solidly know the answer.

4. *Pose your own questions.*

If you're concerned about not getting any questions, be prepared to pose and answer one or two of your own.

If no one has a question at the end of one of my "Presenting with Excellence" seminars, I'll say, "People who attend my workshops often want to know how they can practice good presentation skills in their everyday lives…" And then I suggest three or four things they can do. More often than not, the audience then starts asking questions. If they don't, I pose and answer a second question. I then solicit questions again, using one key additional word: "What _other_ questions do you have about presentation skills?"

You see, no one really wants to be the guinea pig and ask the first question, but once the first question is "out there," the majority of the time, hands start flying up and the Q&A is off and running. If the audience is still silent, I move on to my CTA, but make a note to check with the facility's maintenance staff to see if there's a carbon monoxide leak in the building.

5. *Be proactive.*

If you're fairly certain an unpleasant or off-topic issue is going to come up during Q&A, deal with it proactively.

For example, if a company's benefits manager is speaking about changes to the 401(k) program, very likely some employee is going to stand up during Q&A and complain about the recent poor performance of his portfolio. Instead of waiting for this ~~nut job~~ guy to get on his soapbox, the benefits manager can start the Q&A by framing the discussion and saying, "I'm sure many of you want to ask specific questions about your own portfolios, but in the interests of time and giving the most value to your fellow audience members, let's keep the questions focused only on the upcoming changes. Feel free to see me afterwards or email me your personal questions later."

6. *Be willing to say, "I don't know."*

Most speakers' biggest concern about Q&A sessions is: "What if I don't know the answer to a question?" Go easy on yourself. Your middle name isn't "Google" and no reasonable person should expect you to be a walking Wikipedia®. Plus, audiences are smart enough to know a BS-type smokescreen when they hear one.

Here's my best advice: Go ahead and say "I don't know" or "I don't have that information on hand" and give the questioner a specific date and time when you'll get back to him with the information. Then, be sure to follow through when you said you would. This establishes that you're a person of your word. And here's the cool part: If you say, "I don't know" to a question, you also communicate that you are 100% truthful about the questions you *do* answer.

7. *Let them text you.*
    That's right. This is an especially useful tool with large crowds and younger audiences, where people may not feel as comfortable putting themselves "out there." At the start of your presentation, give out your cell phone number, Google Voice® number (a free service that can be forwarded to any phone), or Twitter username, and encourage your audience to text their questions directly to you. Feel free to answer these questions throughout your talk or field them during a formal Q&A.

    Why would you do this? Because it…
    • allows people to ask questions anonymously.
    • lets you answer questions in the order you prefer.
    • eliminates long-winded, "soap box" questions.
    • lets you sanitize questions before you answer them.
    • stimulates questions throughout the presentation.

    I hate to be the one to break it to you, but believe it or not, some people in your audience are actively checking email and voicemail *during* the presentation. *Gasp!* Why not focus that thumbtastic energy into something constructive related to your talk? The more ways in which you let people communicate with you, the more likely you'll keep their attention and generate a real dialogue.

During Q&A

Repeat or rephrase the question.
It's tempting to start answering a question right away. However, first repeat or rephrase it for your audience. This not only ensures that everyone has heard it, but also allows you to soften any negativity in the original question, if necessary. Additionally, restating or rephrasing buys you time to process what's being asked and to formulate a cogent answer.

Keep your answers concise.
No matter how engaging your presentation was or how much your audience wants the information you're providing, as the end of the meeting approaches, they're ready to get the heck out of Dodge. They have scores of other things on their minds: their next meeting, angry clients, or perhaps a sick loved one at home. When it comes to answering questions, think microwave, not crock-pot.

Try to marry each answer to a key point in your presentation.
For example:

> *Question:* When will this new product be ready for distribution?
>
> *Good answer:* The R130 will be ready for nationwide release in Q3 of next year.

Better answer: The R130 will be ready for nationwide release in Q3 of next year, which means that we will beat our competition to market by at least four months. That's why we need approval for additional funding today in order to stay on pace.

The good answer gets the job done. The better answer does too, but it also reinforces your position and neatly underscores your Call-to-Action.

Taking the Alternate Route

Here's a crazy thought: Consider not having a traditional Q&A session at all. For real. Now, I'm not saying you shouldn't allow your audience to ask questions. While there are certainly some presentation formats, like a keynote speech, that don't include Q&A, that's not what we're discussing here. What I am saying is that questions and answers don't have to occur solely within the limits of the traditional format.

As suggested in idea 7, above, instead of designating time near the end of your speech for questions, invite your audience to ask them (traditionally or via text) throughout the presentation.

The key to pulling this off is knowing your material so well that you can discuss it "out of order" if a query takes you away from your speech's planned trajectory. Also be sure to allow enough time to get through your material with multiple interruptions.

The advantage of this approach, especially in longer presentations, is that it allows a more dynamic exchange of information, transforming a one-sided monologue into a conversation. Plus, if someone has a question early in the talk, he may forget it by the time you finish or tune out until he can ask it. Encouraging Q&A throughout your presentation addresses this head on.

A tweak to the "questions anytime" method is to insert mini Q&A sessions along the way, for example, after every main section of your speech.

Manage Your Audience's Expectations

Regardless of your approach, let your audience know the format for Q&A at the outset of your presentation so that you properly manage their expectations and encourage their input.

Preparation is the key to a great speech. Just don't forget to prepare for the Q&A, too. A little forethought goes a long way toward maximizing your presentation's impact and minimizing your case of nerves.

FAST APP

Before your next presentation, ask yourself: What are the two toughest questions that are most likely to be asked? Then, spend a few minutes thinking through (and writing down) your answers to make sure you have smart, clear, concise responses ready to go. Eliminate the stress before it happens.

Wikipedia is a registered trademark of the not-for-profit Wikimedia Foundation. Google Voice is a registered trademark of Google Inc.

PART TWO:
MAKING IT ENGAGING

10

Great Visuals:
Going Low-Tech for High Impact

A picture is a poem with words.
—Horace, Roman lyric poet

You've probably heard the football expression, "Don't leave the ball on the five yard line." It means you can move the football 95 yards down the length of the field, but if you don't go the final five yards into the end zone, all your efforts won't matter. You won't score any points.

The same goes for presentations. Many well-intentioned, but misguided, speakers think all they need to win over an audience is a solid, well-organized speech with lots of good information. Wrong. Today's audiences are accustomed to unprecedented visual eye candy in their daily lives and naturally expect a certain amount of entertainment (i.e., visual stimulation) in business presentations. Oh sure, they may not openly admit it, but in the back of their minds they're saying, "Wow me."

Part Two of this book is all about the extra ingredients you need to add to your presentation to make it zesty and keep people's attention from SPARQ to CTA.

What Makes a Good Visual Aid?

First, we need to consider what makes a good visual aid.

Adult-learning expert Nan Peck at the Center for Excellence in Teaching and Learning in Annandale, VA, states it this way: "Your visual aids should be big, bold, and brief."[1] This means they should be:

- **Big** enough for *everyone* in the audience to see and read, no matter the size of the room or number of people (e.g., no "eye chart" tables)

- **Bold**, as in dramatic, vibrant, and impactful

- **Brief**, that is, crisp and to-the-point.

Think about the last PowerPoint slide presentation you sat through. Did it pass the big, bold, and brief test? Probably not.

Think Outside the PowerPoint Box

Speaking of PowerPoint, that's what most presenters turn to first when it comes to visual aids. Indeed, the pervasiveness of PowerPoint nowadays—some 40 million presentations daily—has made other visual aids seem prehistoric. However, this can mean a missed opportunity for presenter and listener alike. So before taking up the topic of PowerPoint in the next chapter, I want to make a case for the advantages of other visual media—the ones that don't require electricity.

In fact, good speakers (or, dare I say, *captivating* speakers) employ a variety of visual aids. They know that a mix of presentation media can bring their message alive as opposed to relying on just one format.

Which visual aids should you use? To decide, ask yourself: "Will adding this visual aid improve my presentation?" If the answer is yes, go for it. If the answer is more like: "Maybe, but this is what everybody else does," then you need to think a little harder.

YOU Are the Presentation

However you choose to display your information, keep in mind this very important fact: **YOU ARE THE PRESENTATION.** (All caps? Really? Did I have to yell? YES!) If the focus shifts away from you and your message, your speech loses its punch. Your visual aids and props cannot be the heroes. They're called visual *aids*, not visual replacements. They are meant to support you and make you look good. To be the Robin to your Batman. The Ken to your Barbie. You get the idea.

Options to Consider

Here are some visual aid options to consider beyond PowerPoint:

Flip Charts

Flip charts are the forgotten visual aid, yet they are perfect for small-group presentations. And you don't have to be a Japanese calligrapher or Pablo Picasso to pick up a marker and make your point on an easel. In fact, flip charts work best if the words are brief and the drawings are simple.

One of the benefits of drawing on a flip chart is that it happens live. Audiences quickly become engaged when watching an idea develop in real time. So if you have a simple chart or diagram to explain, create it right in front of their eyes instead of pasting it on a slide.

For example, to illustrate the importance of good verbal transitions between the main points in a speech, I frequently use a flip chart. I start by drawing a stack of three large ovals, representing the sections of a presentation, separated by small spaces (see Figure 10.1). I then add stars between the ovals to show where presenters often become verbal "um" machines as they fumble with what to say when transitioning from one main point to the next. Although this could easily be a static slide, the process of drawing lets the audience feel as though they're discovering the insight with you.

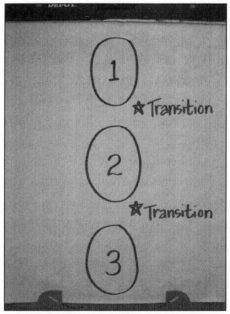

Figure 10.1 — Flip Chart Simplicity.

Using a flip chart to illustrate even one concept while all the rest of your visual aids are on PowerPoint slides can provide a refreshing change of pace in the middle of a presentation.

Two more flip chart tips:

1. To maximize your time, you can sketch parts of your flip chart drawings prior to your meeting. Be sure to write them several pages deep into the flip chart so they remain hidden until you're ready to show them. Then, during the actual presentation, you can add your finishing touches.

2. A good rule of thumb for how big to write on a flip chart is one inch in letter height for every 10 feet of distance between the audience and the easel. Thus, if even one person is seated 25 feet away from the chart, the letters need to be at least 2.5" tall.

Bonus tip: Printed handwriting is easier to read than cursive. *Sorry, Mrs. Walther* (my 3rd grade teacher).

Props

A prop is one of the most powerful ways to bring the content of a speech to life, because it often plays on the unexpected. The possibilities are endless.

Here are a handful of ideas to get you thinking:

• Want to show the cause-and-effect relationships among departments within your company? Line up some dominoes and tip one over. Let the audience see and hear the chain reaction.

- Need to drive home a point about wasteful spending? Hand out play money and ask your audience to tear up their stacks into little pieces. (Take this idea up a notch by walking around with a trashcan and asking people to literally throw their money away.)

- Want to illustrate the riskiness of a potentially unwise acquisition? Roll a pair of dice, deal a few cards, or ask a question to a Magic 8-Ball®.

- How can you underscore the vulnerability of a company's IT system? Bring in a model of a castle, complete with moat and drawbridge, and point out that unwanted "guests" can gain access by other means besides the main gate.

- What if your organization is, strategically speaking, putting all its eggs in one basket? You guessed it. Bring in a basket full of eggs. Believe me, they won't soon forget your point.

- To demonstrate how your organization simply cannot grow without every team member contributing, what about handing out a single puzzle piece to every person in the room?

Demonstrations

A demonstration is basically taking a prop and cranking it up a notch. The greatest demonstration I have personally witnessed was by Hugh Grant. (No, not the handsome British actor. I'm talking about Hugh Grant, the CEO of Monsanto, Inc.)

At Washington University's Olin School of Business, in front of four hundred smartly dressed executives, Mr. Grant illustrated how little of the earth's surface is suitable for growing food for our seven-billion-plus human population. He held up an apple in one hand and a knife in the other. He began by saying, "This apple represents the earth. I'd like you to see how little room we have to work with when it comes to agriculture." As he cut away segments of apple, he would say, "These are the oceans" or "This section represents the deserts and tundra, and we can't grow anything there." When he had finished slicing, a one-sixteenth wedge of the apple remained in his hand. He then said, "Monsanto exists 24/7/365 to maximize *this* part of the apple." He had his audience—yes—eating out of his hand (figuratively speaking, of course).

Some of the first things people think of when it comes to demonstrations are product demos or walking an audience through the pages of a new website. But demonstrations can also be service-oriented, like having a live example of a customer service rep dialoging and problem solving with a customer.

The thing to keep in mind is that your goal is to amplify your information using as many modes as you can—visual, auditory, physical, etc. And if you can invite members of your audience to actively participate in your talk, you open their minds to saying "yes" more readily.

Handouts

Would your point be better illustrated with something that people can touch and hold? A traditional handout, or leave-behind, is like gold to tactile learners. For instance, your handout might contain a diagram for later reference, an org chart with a few empty slots that your attendees fill in during your talk, or a product spec sheet with room for notes. Your call. The key is to make your handout *interactive*, if possible. (For more on handouts, see Chapter 16.)

FAST APP

Once you have outlined your next presentation, take a few minutes to identify the parts or points that need to be brought to life by a stunning, low-tech visual aid. Then get creative. Ask a colleague or friend for ideas if you're stuck.

Magic 8-Ball is a registered trademark of Mattel, Inc.

11

Putting the Power Back into PowerPoint®

My PowerPoint is my best friend. It is my life. I must master it as I master my life...I will learn its weaknesses, its strengths, its fonts, its accessories, its formats and its colors.
—Jack Placke, military humorist

The previous chapter on low-tech visual aids notwithstanding, you may likely be using PowerPoint, or other presentation software like Keynote® or Prezi®, in your presentations. If that's the case, the principles laid out in this chapter are for you.

Let's be clear: I really like PowerPoint. Aside from the microphone, PowerPoint is, without a doubt, the single greatest presentation tool ever invented. It just shouldn't always be your go-to tool if your presentation is better served up in a different way. But when PowerPoint makes sense for you, it can be a phenomenal asset. My beef is with text-heavy, boring, totally predictable PowerPoint presentations that anesthetize and alienate the audience. Or worse, slide presentations that try to mask the speech's shortcomings by using PowerPoint's flashy fonts, cartoon noises, and slide animation schemes. Zing! Boing! Vrrrroooooom! (*Oh, please.* There's a reason Angela Gerber coined the phrase "Death by PowerPoint" in 2001.)

If you are at risk of making such career-limiting PowerPoint mistakes, then these nine slide strategies are for you. Follow them and you'll soon create PowerPoint presentations that truly captivate.

Be a Chef

As I pointed out (okay, shouted) in Chapter 10, YOU, not your visuals, are the presentation. To understand this concept better, think of yourself as a chef. The words and images you flash on the screen are your ingredients. Without you and your expertise, those ingredients are nothing. Your job is to assemble the ingredients and serve them up to the audience right before their eyes, like a teppanyaki chef at Benihana.

If the material on the slide is already "cooked" into a big, wordy display like a prepackaged meal, the chef (presenter) is no longer relevant. With less content on each slide, the speaker remains indispensable as the idea assembler. Call me crazy, but speakers shouldn't write themselves out of their own presentations. Everything in the presentation, especially on your slides, should be *speaker-dependent*.

The point? PowerPoint slides work best if they act like raw ingredients ready to be put together into a dish, rather than fully cooked fare.

So how do you do this? I'll explain.

One Idea per Slide

Part of being a chef is directing the audience's attention to one idea—one dish—at a time. People can process only so much information at once. (That's why American phone numbers were originally limited to seven digits. You can look it up.) So present your listeners with just one clear idea per slide.

Of course, the slide should include enough information to allow your audience to clearly understand what you're trying to communicate. But if you find yourself trying to communicate too much info on a single slide, simply create another slide. There is nothing wrong with having lots of slides in your deck as long as you're serving up the information in bite-sized chunks. "Being a chef" involves keeping your slides simple. One idea per slide allows your audience to focus on and "digest" your material more readily.

The 4x4 Principle

When it comes to text slides, I recommend following the 4x4 Principle:

<u>**The 4x4 Principle**</u>
Use a maximum of four bullet points per slide and no more than four words per bullet point.

Go ahead and faint. I'll wait until you regain consciousness.

This single principle generates the most pushback in my training sessions. Why? Because corporate America has come to rely on slides dripping with text.

Truth be told, speakers have become lazy, using the screen as a giant teleprompter and reading word-for-word, slide after slide. (FYI, this is the #1 complaint from audiences about presenters.)

The problem with putting lots of words on a slide is that an audience can read three to four times faster than a speaker can talk. They are WAY ahead of the speaker and frankly, it's belittling to have someone read out loud to you something that you can read for yourself. So unless you're teaching remedial reading, don't do it.

A far superior tactic is to (a) know your material really well, (b) put just enough words on the screen to remind you of what you want to say, and then (c) face the audience and have a conversation with them. You will connect more deeply. Establish better trust. And generate better acceptance of your ideas.

If you're still not convinced, try using the 4x4 Principle on just a few slides during your next speech. Believe me, your audience will appreciate it, and you will command their attention more fully.

Fonts, Type Size, and Color

When choosing fonts for text slides, people are most comfortable seeing sans serif fonts like Arial® or Helvetica® on the screen. Save your serif fonts (the letters with feet), like Times New Roman® or Garamond™, for your handouts, because people find them easier to read on paper.

Keep the font point size in the 30s or larger, but certainly never under 24. Venturing much below 24 risks making the text illegible for your audience—and it probably means there's too much information on your slide. For the record, the default point sizes in many PowerPoint templates are 44 for the title and 32 for the first level of bullets.

Whatever you do, be sure there's plenty of contrast between the font color and background color—either light text on a dark background or vice versa. Sounds like a no-brainer, yet presenters violate this basic visual principle on a regular basis.

Think Visually

Even though we humans spend most of our day communicating verbally, the fact is, the human brain has an easier time processing images than it does words. Consider, for example, the symbol of a skull and crossbones as the quick read for "poison." And we often find images more illuminating. As an example, residential home listings that include photos earn the seller a $11,500 higher price than listings without pictures.[1]

With this in mind, take a look at each of your text slides and ask, "Can the content on this slide be communicated through a picture or graphic?" Then, let your imagination run wild. The more visuals in your presentation, the better (just one per slide, please). Your audience will love you for it.

For instance, if you're pointing out that a certain department is too isolated from the rest of the organization, why not show a picture of a small island with a single house on it? Or if you're discussing how a new piece of legislation will favor one business over another, show an old-fashioned scale tipped heavily to one side.

The following figures show how a plain, bullet-pointed slide from one of my PowerPoint presentations (Figure 11.1) has been converted into a more impactful image (Figure 11.2).

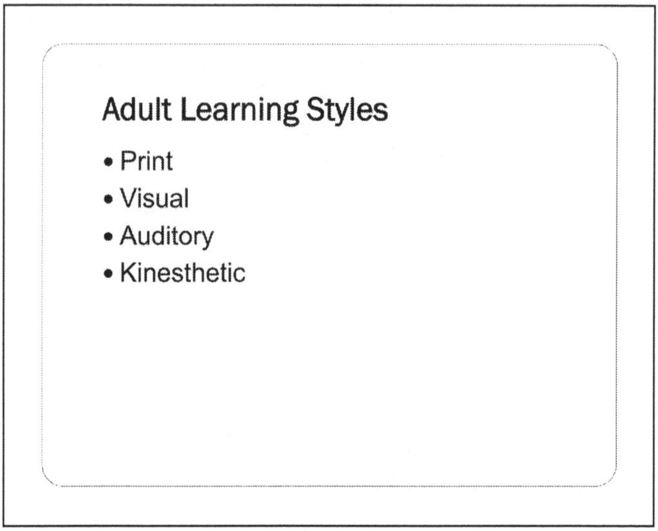

Adult Learning Styles
• Print
• Visual
• Auditory
• Kinesthetic

Figure 11.1 — Before

Adult Learning Styles
Print
Auditory
Visual
Kinesthetic

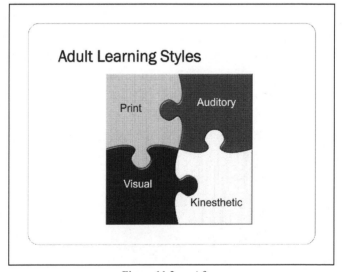

Figure 11.2 — After

To add creative flair to charts and graphs, borrow a page from *USA Today*, which often incorporates icons into its daily factoids. When *USA Today* shows a bar chart about highway funding, for example, the bars are drawn to look like roads, complete with white dashed lines to signify lanes.

I recently helped a dental practice consultancy, Motivations by Mouth (MBM), spruce up a presentation for a national conference. Figure 11.3 shows the original, bullet-pointed text slide. It explains the main reasons people choose to leave a dental practice. A better version, shown in Figure 11.4, uses a bar graph to illustrate these reasons. However, the best version, shown in Figure 11.5, uses a picture of four suitcases of varying heights to bring life to the bar graph. It is a more visually appealing way to illustrate the very same data.

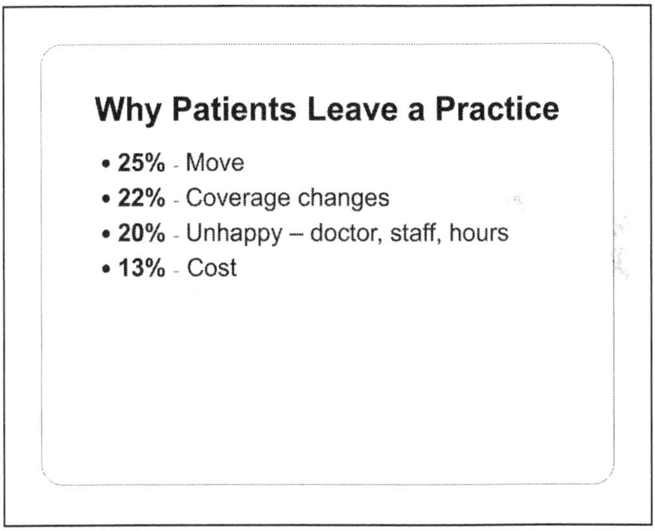

Why Patients Leave a Practice

- **25%** - Move
- **22%** - Coverage changes
- **20%** - Unhappy – doctor, staff, hours
- **13%** - Cost

Figure 11.3 — Why Patients Leave (Original Slide)

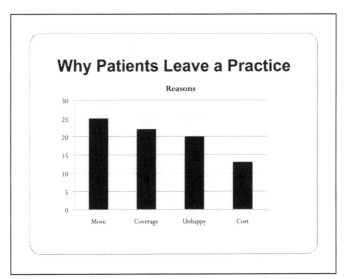

Figure 11.4 — Why Patients Leave (Better)

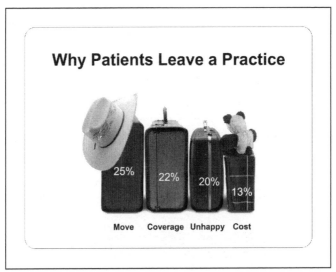

Figure 11.5 — Why Patients Leave (Best)

Using a picture, chart, or graph also helps your presentation become more of a conversation. Why is that? When the speaker is not tied to specific words on the screen, she is freed up to spend most of her time facing the audience. And when you are conversing face-to-face with the audience, they're engaged—which means they're more willing to buy into what you're saying. Not a bad way to spend an hour.

Slide Variety

While visually stunning slides are important, variety across your slideshow (or slide "deck") is critical. Again, this addresses how our brains are wired. We tune out whatever is boring or expected and lock in on things that are intriguing or different. For our stimulus-hungry brains, a steady stream of similar-looking slides is an invitation to start thinking about something more interesting, like tonight's dinner or remembering to pick up our dry cleaning. The solution? Give your audience variety and keep them stimulated.

To assess the amount of variety within your slide deck, put on your director's hat and take a tip from Steven Spielberg: Storyboard your presentation. Switch the view in PowerPoint from "Outline" to "Slide Sorter" so you can see a 30,000-foot view of many or all of your slides at one time. Consider the mix of text, images, and graphs in your deck. If you see too many of one kind of slide format or one section seems to drag, consider changing a slide or two to a different layout. One easy fix is to employ PowerPoint's SmartArt Graphics with its bevy of ready-made graphs just waiting for your touch.

While there's no magic slide mixture formula to guarantee a successful presentation, variety always helps. It's not just the spice of life, it's also the best hedge against predictability and boredom.

Highlight What's Important

Whether you use text or graphics, the audience's attention needs to zero in easily on the most salient part(s) of each slide. Ask yourself: What is the audience supposed to learn via this slide? What should they look at first? Then, emphasize that information using color, italics, bold text, a bright circle, an arrow, a callout bubble, or whatever works best. Any of these can easily be added to a slide with just a few clicks of the mouse.

Animation Schemes

I can count on one hand the number of times during my two decades in advertising and professional speaking when I've seen a speaker successfully use animation in a PowerPoint presentation. It's just not necessary. In fact, most of the time animation is used because the speech itself is brain-meltingly boring and the presenter thinks animated objects or sounds will make up for it. It's like trying to mask the flavor of bad meat by dousing it with seasoning. Good luck with that.

If you feel tempted to animate your slides, ask yourself, "Will animation make the information on my slide easier to understand?" If the answer is "no," don't do it. If it's "yes," animate, but tread lightly.

The only "Steve approved" animation is PowerPoint's build feature, which adds bulleted items to the screen one line at a time with the click of the remote. Otherwise, let's leave the animation to the geniuses at Disney-Pixar.

Transitions and Sound Effects

Like animation schemes, clever transitions between slides are unnecessary. You know what I'm talking about—the checkerboard, the wipe-away, the pixilated dissolve, etc. They're usually cheesy in nature, and all of them distract from your message.

What about sound effects? Here's my friendly tip: Don't use them. How in the world will a thunderclap make your material easier to understand? (The one exception might be a speech about meteorology.) Instead, craft a great presentation, tell a good story, and use strong visuals that don't require noises.

To Wrap Up

I'll take my own advice and show you instead of telling you: Figure 11.6 wraps this chapter up in classic 4x4 style.

Above all, remember: YOU are the presentation. Make your slides 100% speaker-dependent, and your presentation will shine.

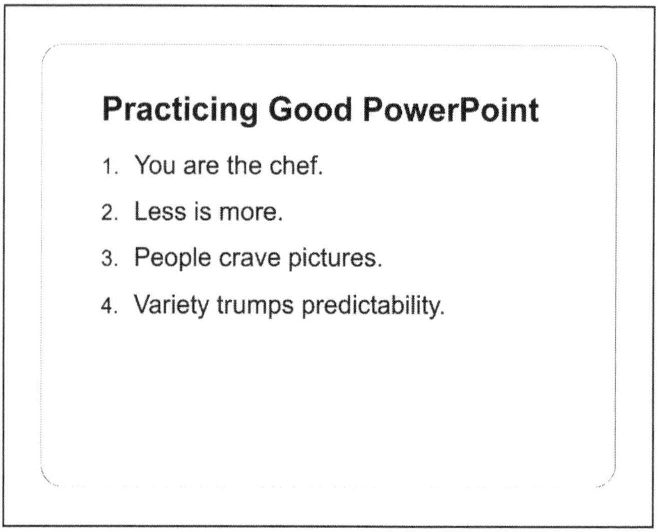

Practicing Good PowerPoint

1. You are the chef.

2. Less is more.

3. People crave pictures.

4. Variety trumps predictability.

Figure 11.6 — Classic 4x4 Slide

FAST APP

After assembling your PowerPoint presentation, switch to the "Slide Sorter" view and look at the entire sweep of slides. What do you see? Lots of text? Eye-catching pictures? Is there color or is it monochromatic?

Ask yourself which slides could be improved by doing one of these four things:

1. Convert words to images.

2. Add color.

3. Replace a bullet slide with a graph or schematic.

4. Replace a slide or two with low-tech visual aids (see Chapter 10). (Kind of a weird way to end a chapter on PowerPoint, but somebody had to say it.)

12

Finding and Telling Good Stories

If history were taught in the form of stories,
it would never be forgotten.

—Rudyard Kipling,
Nobel Prize-winning author

If good data and straight facts were enough to persuade an audience, then all you'd have to do in your presentation is hand out a spreadsheet and say, "There! Are we all in agreement?" Not so fast, my friend. In order to be effective, the way in which your information is presented must capture attention and be memorable. So, to add some sizzle to your next presentation, start by finding and telling great stories.

Why Stories?

Stories are, without a doubt, one of the most powerful tools in your communication arsenal. In fact, a study published in *Scientific American*[1] shows that people remember both stories and illustrations better than a straightforward presentation of facts. If you can tie your key point or message to a story, your audience is more likely to listen and recall what you said long after the presentation ends.

Think about the best business presentations, political speeches, or keynote addresses you've ever heard. Chances are, the specific facts have long since faded, but the stories you heard to reinforce those facts have stayed with you.

Why are stories so effective? We humans have been sharing stories since we started drawing on cave walls. You might say stories are hardwired into our DNA. Jerome S. Bruner, cofounder of the Center for Cognitive Studies at Harvard University, puts it this way: "Humans have an inherent readiness or predisposition to organize experience into story form: into viewpoints, characters, intentions, sequential plot structures, and the rest."

Here's what stories do:

- Stories give life to your facts.
- Stories help you deliver uncomfortable truths in a palatable way.
- Stories reach across gender, race, religion, nationality, and creed.
- Stories are easy to remember. This means they are easy to tell. (Really.)
- For the same reason, stories are retold.
- Stories are fun, so they keep your audience engaged.
- Stories open minds in a nonthreatening manner.
- Stories lift spirits.

Nine Tips for Telling a Good Story

Here are nine pointers on how to take advantage of this powerful tool in your next talk:

1. *Have a point.*
    Identify the key idea you're trying to communicate. For
    instance, is it change, opportunity, inspiration, potential
    danger, a desirable goal?

2. *Match your point to a story.*
    Find a story that illustrates that idea. Stories are inherently
    entertaining, but telling a story for the story's sake won't
    fly. As long as your audience sees the connection between
    your story and the point you're making, they will gladly
    come along for the ride.

3. *Keep the story brief.*
    As much as people love to hear stories, keep in mind this is
    not the National Storytelling Festival in Jonesborough,
    Tennessee. A good business story is relatively quick—so
    tell it and move on. It can be as short as three or four
    sentences or several minutes long. But remember, shorter is
    better. (For more information on the Festival, as well as on
    the art of storytelling, visit www.storytellingcenter.net.)

4. *Set the scene.*
    Identify the story's place and time. Introduce the
    characters, making clear why each is involved. Provide
    enough detail to set up the story's action, but no more.

5. *Get to the conflict early.*
    Unlike telling a story at your local Starbuck's or the office
    water cooler, in a business presentation it's best to get to
    the drama of the story quickly. Too much buildup, and the
    audience will grow restless.

6. *Add tension and build to a climax.*
    As you establish the conflict or obstacle, be sure to infuse your story with drama and get your audience wondering, "How will this ever work out?" This is what separates a story from a news report or a straight recitation of the facts.

7. *Whenever possible, tell the story in the present tense.*
    Relating a story in the present tense enhances its immediacy and brings it to life.

8. *Connect the story to the point.*
    Be sure to connect the story to the point you are making. Think of it as stating the moral of the story. (You don't necessarily have to state it openly. Sometimes it's best to let the audience infer the meaning on their own.)

9. *Link the story to your listeners.*
    The best storytellers use rhetorical questions based on the story to get the audience thinking about how the story relates to them. Trainers call this concept "learning transfer."

The Frappuccino® Bar

Here's a story that I often tell in my workshops. In this instance, I'm using it to underscore the importance of being flexible and taking life's obstacles in stride. Notice how it incorporates the aspects of a good story, above.

One of the first business trips of my career started off well, but nearly ended in disaster.

I was in my mid-20s, working at a sales promotion agency on several large national accounts. After working remotely with a new client for nearly six months, my team and I fly out to San Francisco for a huge presentation.

We arrive in the Bay Area around noon—just in time for the client's annual outdoor employee barbeque. Cool. Before meeting the key people on the client team, we're invited to grab a burger, a cup of lemonade, and a patch of grass next to their building. The food is delicious and it's fun to see the CEO wearing an apron and flipping burgers.

Right before the picnic ends, someone announces, "Hey, everybody! Come get your Starbuck's Frozen Frappuccino Bar!" Now, having never heard of these bars, but loving Frappuccinos, I immediately make my way to the giant portable coolers. I reach in, grab a bar, unsheathe it, and put it in my mouth.

Unbeknownst to me, in order to keep the Frappuccino Bars cold, the food service provider has used dry ice—which has a surface temperature of 109°F below zero. And my Frappuccino Bar must have been sitting directly on a chunk of dry ice for several hours, because the moment it hits my mouth, it flash freezes to my top lip, my bottom lip, and my tongue. And I cannot get it to budge.

Knowing that in a few minutes my body heat will melt a fraction of the bar's surface and set me free, I don't panic. But just then, one of my team members says, "Steve, c'mon let's go. The meeting's starting right now."

Now I panic. Just for the record, it's hard to make a great first impression if you mumble your name and refuse to remove foodstuffs from your mouth. Still, I walk proudly into that meeting room, smile (as best I can), and offer firm handshakes to everyone present.

The client says, "My, Steve, you've taken quite a fancy to that Frappuccino Bar." I nod in response, smiling oafishly around the bar that's still frozen solid to my mouth, and remain uncharacteristically quiet for the first part of the meeting. In fact, I begin to sweat, wondering how long I can get by with just smiling, nodding, and saying, "Um-humph."

Well...eventually the bar works its way free, I explain what happened, and we all have a good laugh about it. And in case you're wondering, the meeting was a smashing success.

[And now I apply the story to the topic at hand.]

As you think about the recent restructuring of your department, how did you handle some of the unexpected challenges you encountered? We're constantly faced with obstacles, but it's the way we respond that makes us a better organization...

The great part about stories is that they can apply to a myriad of situations. There are several other points I could have addressed when using this story. Here are a few:

1. The need for patience
2. The benefits of taking a long-term view of things
3. That "One-Step-at-a-Time" can solve problems (or in this case, one lip at a time)
4. Know what you're getting yourself into.

5.   Be prepared for when things go wrong.

This story takes less than two minutes to tell, yet it's one that audiences remember long after the presentation. So they're more likely to recall the point I'm making.

Now What?

Start collecting stories.

Borrow a page from the late Hall of Fame professional speaker, Zig Ziglar, who read the local newspaper cover-to-cover every day looking for useful stories and anecdotes. If the newspaper is too old school, then indulge in a bounty of online sources— blogs, news sites, etc. Either way, the point is to be looking daily, or at least often. Stories show up in extraordinary places.

There are many other story sources: story books, story sites, story organizations, and of course, the stories you hear in everyday conversation. Reportedly, writer Aaron Sorkin wrote the play (and eventually the movie) "A Few Good Men" after hearing about a Marine incident at a cocktail party. The key is to begin stockpiling your favorites. Sources for some of my best stories include the "Letters to the Editor" section of a weekly news magazine, the CEO of AT&T at an alumni event, my brother-in-law over Thanksgiving turkey, and a History Channel program on the Middle Ages. Go figure.

Sometimes the best stories come from your own personal experience. Stories from your own life are easy to relate because you know the events so well. Plus, they're 100% original, which keeps your presentations fresh.

A Few Other Suggestions

Here are a few other suggestions as you build your story collection:

Write it down.
When you come across a great story, write it down, even if you're not sure when or where you'll use it. Write down the bare bones—context, characters, conflict, key facts, and the point it communicates. Several speakers I know use recorded voice memos on their smartphones to capture important details. Note the source, too. Or, just jot down the website, journal issue, or other reference so you can return to the story when you have more time.

Flesh it out.
Later, take a few minutes to flesh out the story from your notes or smartphone, writing it out in enough detail to enable you to retell it when the time comes. Writing it out helps in recalling details, and a story once written out is easier to deliver from memory in front of an audience. (Note: This is different than scripting out your speech word-for-word. Why? Because specific words and turns of phrase are more important in stories. Plus, we are more accustomed to telling stories in everyday life, which makes memorizing them and re-playing them effortless. Whereas, people who try to give entire speeches from memory often sound stilted and robotic.)

Set up a story file.
A story file is just a central place where you keep and organize your stories. Even consider setting up two story files: a physical

one for magazine and newspaper clippings, newsletters, etc., and one on your computer to house your written stories and links to stories online.

Sort your stories.

As your story collection grows, periodically take a few minutes to sort stories into categories according to the points they illustrate. It will then be easier to find the right story quickly when you're crafting a presentation.

Be a storyteller. Start using stories in your speeches and watch what happens. Most likely your audience will lean forward and pay closer attention to what you're saying and then you can marvel at how much better your recommendations are received.

The following **FAST APP** will get you started by helping you add anecdotes and stories from your own life to your collection.

FAST APP

Catalog the stories from your own life. Jot down, in stream-of-consciousness style, a list of stories you have told over the years, lessons you've learned, things that happened to you as a kid, in college (keep it G-rated), experiences you've had while traveling, or "ah-ha" moments from everyday experiences. Consider including stories from your family's collective history or stories from friends, too. For the moment, don't worry about what points these stories could illustrate. That comes later. You'll be surprised how much material you're able to generate.

For this exercise to work properly, give it a good 15–20 minutes of uninterrupted time. No music in the background. Turn off the cell phone. Close out of email. Just let things flow and see where your mind takes you.

Frappuccino is a registered trademark of Starbucks Corporation.
Sadly, I think those delicious frozen Frappuccino bars may no longer be available.
Ah, well, I'll always have San Francisco.

13

Other Ways to Spice Up Your Talk

Predictability is the killer of attention.
—Roy H. Williams,
best-selling author, marketing expert

Stories are awesome, but they're certainly not the only way to add interest to a presentation. Thought-provoking quotations, arresting pictures, powerful analogies, and even *New Yorker* cartoons can also do the trick. (Do these sound familiar? They should. They're elements of the SPARQ discussed in Chapter 7. And they're just as useful throughout your speech.)

Where Art Thou, Oh Illustration?

People often ask me (and by often, I mean at least twice), "Where can I find really good pictures or quotes for my presentations? I have no clue where to start." I tell them it's not a matter of where to look. Material for spicing up your next presentation is everywhere. It's just a matter of adjusting your antennae to see it.

Think back to the last time you bought a car. The instant you made up your mind to enter the auto market, you probably started noticing dealerships you hadn't noticed before. You paid attention to car commercials and billboards for cars you had previously ignored. The same is true for finding material to enliven your speech. The moment you decide to look, you'll begin to see great material everywhere.

Once you identify something great, the next step is to capture it. You do this by acting like a reporter.

Act Like a Journalist

Do you know what Thomas Edison, Walt Whitman, and Ludwig van Beethoven had in common? No, they weren't journalists. All three carried a notebook with them everywhere they went. They understood that ideas come to us at all times of the day, and the only way to capture them is to jot them down the moment they present themselves. It's a great lesson for speakers.

Today, nearly everyone has a smartphone or iPad® with them 24/7, making it possible to not only capture thoughts and ideas, but also to take pictures and make quick audio recordings. Personally, I'm an iPhone® guy. Scores of apps are available on the App Store for capturing and cataloging "info bits."

One of my favorite examples of serendipitous picture taking was the shot I took of a FedEx drop box located *inside* the U.S. Post Office in the lobby of the Aon Center in downtown Chicago. Really. (See Figure 13.1). The photo is a fantastic example of using your competitor's strengths to your advantage; that is, "If you can't beat 'em, join 'em."

Figure 13.1 — FedEx Drop Box Inside U.S. Post Office

Finding Nuggets – The Quick & Easy Way

Finding material does not have to take a lot of time. Again, just go about your normal, everyday life and capture what you see, hear, or read as it happens.

Or, you can proactively dedicate a few minutes to gathering fantastic material from the comfort of your office chair.

Situation:

It's Tuesday morning, 9:55 A.M. (you pick the month and date). You have five minutes before a departmental meeting begins. What can you do with this time?

a.   Answer email.
b.   Make a quick phone call.
c.   Organize your desk (i.e., move things from one stack to another).
d.   Stroll over to a colleague's office and talk about your weekend plans.
e.   Do some research for next week's big presentation.
f.   All of the above.

If you answered "f," it's time for a vacation.

While all of these are valid options, let's explore "e" and see what kind of serious research can be done in five minutes. Besides online auctions, dating sites, and fantasy football leagues, did you know the Internet can also be used to find juicy statistics, great quotes, and amazing images? Instead of thinking you have to carve out two or three hours to do this research (which will never happen), just chip away at it one piece at a time.

It's important to mention here that you can't simply download whatever you'd like from the Internet and slap it into your presentation without properly attributing it to its owner. Beyond giving proper credit to the source, also be sure to check carefully for any usage requirements (e.g., permission from the author or a fee) or restrictions regarding the material you'd like to use—be it an image, video, comic strip, or other item— prior to usage and make sure you are in compliance with them.

Following are lists of websites to help get you started. *(Note: These sites and the information on them can and do change.)*

Quotations
- www.thinkexist.com - more than 300,000 quotations searchable by author or topic
- www.great-quotes.com – over 54,000 quotes
- www.bartleby.com – 11,000 literary quotes (click on Bartlett's Quotations)
- www.quoteland.com – thousands of quotes searchable by category
- www.brainyquote.com – another great quote resource

A cool way to find off-the-beaten-path quotations not cataloged on traditional quote sites is to type the key words in quotation marks plus the word "quote" into your favorite search engine. Example: "_____ _____" + quote. This technique will yield interesting quotes that lie outside of the major quote sites.

Pictures
Free Sites
- www.google.com (Google Images) – These are free images, BUT YOU MUST GET PERMISSION FROM THE OWNER BEFORE USING AN IMAGE; otherwise, it's stealing.
- www.creativecommons.org - a good site for royalty-free content (also has usage requirements)
- www.pixabay.com – free images on a large database with an interesting name
- www.freepik.com - thousands of free images you can use as long as you give proper attribution

Pay-Per-Image Sites
- www.123rf.com – great downloadable images for $1, $2, or $3 apiece
- www.istockphoto.com – royalty-free pictures for $1 to $15 per image
- www.photos.com – large image database; for a monthly fee, users can download as many royalty-free images as they like
- www.gettyimages.com – selections from top photographers; some of the best pictures you'll find anywhere and they're priced accordingly

Cartoons
- www.cartoonbank.com – access to every *New Yorker* comic strip ever printed; users can download individual comic strips (roughly $20/year for unlimited use of a single comic strip in your presentations)
- www.kingfeatures.com – similar to Cartoon Bank, this site offers a vast assortment of comic strips, from *Amazing Spiderman* to *Zits*; users can download comic strips (approximately $20/year per comic)

Let Google Do the Work
Google Alerts™ (www.Google.com/Alerts) is a free service that sends daily or weekly email updates to your inbox on a chosen topic. For instance, if you're interested in creative ways to reward employees, you can set up a Google Alert for "employee rewards" or "creative employee recognition." When an article, news item, or blog post using those words hits the Internet, you'll receive a Google Alert, with links to the info.

Start a "Cool Things" File

Similar to a story file, you can create a "Cool Things" file on your computer for the interesting tidbits you collect. Also set up a physical file for hardcopy items—articles, pictures, cartoons, and those handwritten notes you scribble on napkins when electronic devices are not an option, like during takeoffs and landings (and traffic school). As with collecting stories, eventually you'll have enough material to organize into categories. Currently I have the following folders: Stories, Great Quotes, Pictures, plus a "Cool Things" file for everything else.

The Speech-Worthy Test

The other question I'm often asked about finding really good material is: "How do I know if what I'm collecting is any good for a presentation?" Weigh it against these questions:

Did it...
- Surprise you?
- Make you laugh?
- Make you think?
- Stir your emotions?
- Stop you in your tracks?

If you answer "yes" to any of these, then throw it into your file.

Having a wide assortment of illustrations on-hand to add flavor to your presentations is like an insurance policy. You need to have insurance in place *before* you experience a problem (in this case, livening up your speech). In other words, just gather as much stuff as you can. Don't worry about when or where to use it. We'll get to that in Chapter 15 when we explore matchmaking.

FAST APP

1. Grab a manila folder and label it "Cool Things" or "Illustrations" or...you pick the title.
2. Get a notepad app for your smartphone or iPad to capture stories and ideas as you encounter them. If old school works better for you, take a cue from Thomas Edison and carry a small notebook with you at all times. (I like the pocket-sized Moleskine® notebooks.)
3. Be ready to snap a picture at a moment's notice for homegrown presentation images (or for when you spot a celebrity).
4. Start collecting!

---

iPad and iPhone are registered trademarks of Apple Inc.
Google Alerts is a trademark of Google Inc.
Moleskine is a registered trademark of Moleskine SpA.

14

Leave 'Em Laughing:
Adding (Appropriate) Humor

Once you get people laughing, they're listening
and you can tell them almost anything.
—Herb Gardner, playwright, film director

Humor is like dynamite. When used properly, humor can clear tunnels through mountains of resistance and move a presentation forward in a powerful way. But when it's used as a gimmick to get a cheap laugh, it can blow up in the presenter's face (and really mess up your hair), i.e., the speaker's credibility will take a hit.

For this and a host of other reasons, many professionals are reluctant to use humor in business settings.

Here are the top nine reasons why presenters shy away from using humor:

1. I won't be funny.
2. I might offend someone.
3. I'll botch the punch line.
4. My audience won't get it.
5. I will come across as unprofessional.
6. I'm about as funny as a dinner plate (i.e., I don't have a sense of humor.)

7. I have so much information to convey that there's no room in my speech to add humor.
8. I've never used humor in the past. (If I start now, people might think I'm off my meds.)
9. I lead a fairly unfunny life. Even if I wanted to add laughter to a speech, I have no idea where to find humorous material.

Make Sure It's Relevant

The above are all valid concerns. The main way to overcome them is to make sure your humor is directly relevant to your material. What does this mean?

Keep in mind that you're speaking to a group to convey an idea or achieve a particular goal. Nothing should be included in your speech that doesn't help you reach that goal.

Humor is no different. The only recommended (i.e., safe) use of humor in a presentation is to help you accomplish your objective. In other words, humor isn't just a cheap way to liven up a talk; it's a serious communication tool.

Serious Subjects and Humor

Another reason people hesitate to use humor is that they think their particular subject matter is so unique or serious that there just isn't any humorous material out there related to their subject matter. Not true. Something humorous can relate to your presentation without being *literally* related to your subject matter.

Let me give you an example. A few years ago, I was asked to help a group of 60 partners at a big law firm in Chicago add more humor (and humanity) to their presentations. Near the end of the program, one of the lawyers stood up and said rather skeptically, "I give speeches on banking law reform. Trust me, I've looked everywhere for humorous stories, quotes, and cartoons that deal with banking law reform. There just aren't any." (Hmm, that's surprising. You'd think there'd be an entire section at Barnes & Noble labeled "Funny Things about Banking Law Reform.")

After asking this fine attorney a few questions, we identified that the key message in most of his speeches was the idea of *change* or *dealing with change*. "That's it!" I cried. Trying to find specific humorous content about banking law reform was a dead end. All he needed was funny stuff on the topic of change, which is easy to find.

Here are several ways he could add some levity to his talks on banking law reform:

Use a Quotation
"Change is inevitable – except from a vending machine."
–Robert C. Gallagher

Show a *New Yorker* cartoon
The cartoon features a man in a hotel room getting a wake-up call from the front desk. He has a concerned look on his face, and the voice on the other end of the phone is saying: "This is your wake-up call. – Change or die."

After using either of the above, our banking law attorney could link it to his topic:

"The reason I bring this up is to highlight the changes we're seeing in the world of banking..."

Or...

Tell a Quick (3-Sentence) Story:
Many years ago, two salesmen were sent by a British shoe manufacturer to a remote part of the globe to investigate and report back on market potential.
The first salesman reported back:
"There is no potential here.— Nobody wears shoes."
The second salesman reported back:
"There is massive potential here.— Nobody wears shoes."

To tie this bit of humor into his topic, the attorney could then say something like:
"The recent changes we've seen in banking laws present us with an opportunity to be like that second salesman and find ways to see the upside of the new legislation."

It's as simple as that.

The Science of Humor – Why It Works

What makes humor such a potent communication tool? In a nutshell, the laughter that results from humor makes us feel good, and an audience that feels good is generally more open to what the speaker has to say. As Martha Stewart is fond of saying, "That's a good thing."

Why does laughter make us feel good? Scientific studies confirm that laughter brings about a host of physiological benefits, including improved circulation, better respiration, a boost to the immune system, and, best of all, the release of endorphins.[1] I won't bother you with all the science. Just know that endorphins are the chemical cousins of morphine. When they are released in your brain, you get a temporary happy boost—a perfectly safe and legal chemical party in your noggin. Sign me up.

Other Benefits to Your Presentation

Humor used correctly in a presentation offers scores of other benefits besides giving the audience a lift. It also:

- Increases the speaker's likeability.
- Brings people together and facilitates group problem solving[2].
- Sparks interest in the subject matter.
- Helps you and your material to be more memorable.
- Opens people's minds to new ideas, and to new connections between ideas, in a non-threatening way.

Finally, if a speaker is willing to use humor to poke fun at himself, he demonstrates confidence and shows that he doesn't take himself too seriously. Further, self-deprecating humor makes you more accessible and likeable to the audience. Just don't overdo it with self-deprecating wit, however. A comment or two is fine, but anything more feels like a cry for help. (That's what therapists are for.)

With the science on your side, why not consider using a bit of humor to help win over your next audience?

A Handful of Humor Pointers

Here are some additional tips that will help you decide how and when to incorporate humor into your next presentation.

- **Tell stories, not jokes.**
  According to the *New York Times*, the standard joke (which begins with something like, "A lawyer, an accountant, and a duck walk into a bar....") is no longer culturally relevant. It died in the spring of 2005.[3] Rest in peace.

- **Take a tip from the pros: Use tested material.**
  David Letterman had at least 10 different writers submit their own "Top 10 List" every night for his show. From that pool of 100+ ideas, he selected the 10 funniest and, even then, there were usually one or two that weren't all that funny. It's risky to try to be funny with original material. There's no need to write your own stuff when you can borrow (with attribution) from the mountains of humorous material already out there. Exception: If you use humor quite a bit in your everyday life and it's a natural extension of who you are, then by all means, go for it and try out some original material. But for the rest of us, there's no need to reinvent the wheel.

- **When something goes wrong during your talk, acknowledge it out loud.**
  Sometimes the funniest stuff comes from our unfettered, organic reaction to things that happen during a presentation. Your ad-libbed remark may be funny, but even when it isn't, you'll be voicing what the audience is

already thinking, which deepens your connection with them.

- *Choose humor that is consistent with your personality and style.*
  If you're laid back, don't try something over-the-top. People will think you've had one too many Red Bulls®. If you're high-energy and outgoing, subtle one-liners will seem out of place.

- *Be brief.*
  As comedian Steve Roye says, "Get to the funny fast." People will give you a certain amount of leeway with humor, but they'll grow impatient with a five-to-seven minute diversion from your speech. Be like a Navy SEAL.— Get in, take care of business, and get out. (By the way, I'm pretty sure that's not the Navy SEAL motto, but it ought to be.)

- *Stay on topic.*
  The two deadliest words ever uttered in a speech are "but seriously." They're an admission that you just tried to tell a funny joke or story that was absolutely unrelated to the presentation and a waste of your audience's valuable time. Don't go there.

- *Don't be off-color.*
  It's hard to believe that, in the twenty-first century, the following needs to be said, yet it does: No professional business presentation should ever include a joke about ethnicity, gender, religion, sex, national origin, or a similar topic. Such humor is not funny. You'll end up offending

someone, you'll look foolish in the process, and you can expect a call from HR when you get back to your desk.

- ***Don't be late for dinner.***
  (This just seemed to fit. Plus, it's good manners.)

Is using humor in a speech risky? You bet. However, if you make your humor relevant to your topic, use clean and vetted material, and keep it short, you'll look like a comedy genius. While you may never get your own sitcom, your customers, co-workers, and prospects will appreciate your effort and enjoy the presentation more. Or, as we say in the National Speakers Association:

Question: "Should you use humor in your speeches?"
Answer: "Only if you want to get paid."

FAST APP

Get a notes app on your smartphone if you don't already have one. Then, throughout the day, make a note of anything that makes you laugh or smile, as well as anything you said that made others laugh.

Record the scene: What was going on? What did you say? How did the humor come about?

Put these vignettes and observations into a file, because they just might be the right prescription for a much-needed endorphin rush in the middle of your next talk.

Red Bull is a registered trademark of Red Bull.

15

Matchmaking

When we try to pick out anything by itself,
we find it hitched to everything else in the universe.
—John Muir, naturalist, explorer

Once those files of stories and illustrations begin to grow, you're ready for the really fun part. I call it "matchmaking."

As you put together your next presentation, take a look at your Take-Home Message. Are you introducing a new product? Educating junior staff on operational standards? Selling your firm to a prospect? Whatever it is, look through your notes app, your pocket notebook, or your "Cool Things" or "Stories" file to find stories, anecdotes, quotes, or pictures that match the points you're trying to communicate. It's that simple.

If you don't find a great example in your files, don't panic. In addition to doing a quick Google search, seek out a co-worker or two (especially ones who are outside your area/department) to help you come up with some fresh ideas. Many times, we get so close to our material that we can't see beyond the usual examples or low-hanging fruit. Remember, every idea in a brainstorming session is a possibility and sometimes the most ridiculous "I could never say that" idea is the one that sparks a real breakthrough.

There's no magic mix of anecdotes, pictures, quotes, etc. Just go by gut feel (unless you had the 5-alarm chili for lunch). The goal is to strike a balance between elements to keep your audience engaged and cement your points in their minds. A good blend of elements will keep the material fresh and exciting for you, as well. And if you enjoy it, your audience will, too.

Mix Business with Pleasure

You've, no doubt, heard the expression, "Don't mix business with pleasure." I disagree when it comes to public speaking. When done correctly, you can not only mix business with pleasure, but you can also leverage the combination to your advantage.

For example, I recently coached an executive at a large electrical supply company tasked with giving a "state of the industry" presentation at a national conference. Even though he loved what he did for a living, he struggled mightily to generate enthusiasm for this speech. His first draft was flat, lifeless, and way too businessy (yes, that's a word). And he delivered it with all the enthusiasm of a teenager on garage cleaning day.

When I asked what he liked to do in his spare time, his eyes lit up and a smile came over his face. He loved fly-fishing. If it were humanly possible, he would fish 24/7. "Great!" I said. "Can you think of ways that the current business climate for electrical distributors is similar to fly-fishing?" After 10 minutes of think time he came up with several interesting analogies, like:

- Finding areas of the river that have not been "fished over" = being creative in finding new customers
- Seeking out undiscovered rivers = looking for new revenue streams
- Getting the best lures, fishing line, and rod on the market = upgrading back-office equipment

Same facts as before, same business situation, but connecting what he loved to do with what he had to say turned him into an enthusiastic presenter. Audience members at the conference reported that he knocked it out of the park. Many could not recall a more enjoyable state of the industry speech. In this fish story, the big one didn't get away.

Real-World Example: Your Company Is Stuck in a Rut and Reluctant to Change

Let's say you're making a presentation next week in which you will recommend that your company makes a major change, and soon, or serious financial trouble will loom. The company has a history of doing things "the way we've always done them."

Here are four ways in which you could help them see the need for change:

Solution 1:
Revise Their Outlook with a Story

Four big-game hunters are taking their annual trip to a remote area in the Canadian wilderness to hunt elk. The small seaplane that dropped them off at the beginning of the trip returns a week later to pick them up. Each hunter has snared a large elk.

The pilot says, "I'm sorry, guys, but the load-bearing weight limits of this plane will only hold the four of you, your gear, and two elk. The other two elk will have to stay behind."

One of the hunters becomes enraged and says, "Last year each of us had a similar-sized elk, the same gear, and we were in the same kind of plane that you're flying today. We're not leaving without all four elk."

The pilot acquiesces. They all pile into the plane and take off. But shortly after takeoff, they start losing altitude and crash.

As they pull themselves from the wreckage, one of the hunters says to the other, "Do you have any idea where we are?"

His buddy replies, "I think we're about a mile from where we crashed last year."

The moral of the story? You can't keep doing the same thing and expect to get different results.

Solution 2:
Open Their Minds with a Quote

- "Even if you're on the right track, you'll get run over if you just sit there." —Will Rogers
- "Long-term planning is not about making long-term decisions, it is about understanding the future consequences of today's decisions." —Gary Ryan Blair
- "Talk doesn't cook rice." —Chinese proverb

Solution 3:
Show a Picture of a Bright (or Dismal) Future

Flash a picture of a run-down gas station on the screen.

Let the image settle in their minds for three or four seconds and then say, "Our situation today reminds me of this gas station, which was doing a fine business along Route 66. Customers were plentiful and the station was profitable, but that was 40 or 50 years ago. One day something interesting happened. The interstate was rerouted and moved 15 miles north. Cars stopped coming by. The gas station owners stayed right where they were, thinking everything would be fine and hoping that travelers would happily drive 15 miles off the interstate to gas up. However, that didn't happen. Their business model was unsustainable and today there's nothing left but broken glass, cracked concrete, and rusted pumps.

[And then pivot back to the problem at hand.]

"Ladies and gentlemen, we're meeting today because *our* highway has moved, in the form of _____ [fill in the blank]. And if we don't take action soon, we'll find ourselves in a similar predicament. Today we're going to explore three ideas on how we can turn this situation to our advantage."

By the way, I found several great pictures of run-down gas stations on a 27-second Google Images™ search. After securing the owner's permission, I've used the image of an old gas station along Route 66 to illustrate the above point in dozens of presentations. (See Figure 15.1.)

Solution 4:
Ask a Future-Oriented Question
Whatever the date of your presentation, select the same date one to five years in the future and say, "Imagine it's now [name that future month, day, and year] and our company has failed to achieve every revenue goal we had set. What do you think got in our way?"

After a moment's pause say, "Now imagine that it's [the same month, day, and year] and we've achieved every financial goal we'd set. What do you think made the difference?"

Figure 15.1 – Gas Station Goes Under Because Highway Has Moved.

Here are three other questions you could ask to generate the same kind of engagement:

- "If time were no object, how could we better serve our clients?"
- "How would our business look if we did not have this [current issue] staring us in the face?"
- "If we had all the resources in the world, how could we eliminate this obstacle?"

Creative elements that set-up or solidify your main points can spell the difference between your audience paying attention and having them zone out, which can mean the difference between success and failure. All you have to do is match the idea you're trying to communicate to the resources you've gathered.

How many stories or illustrations are needed? A good rule of thumb is one for every major point in the presentation (and by major point, I mean the three to four points you use to support your Take-Home Message). It's always better to have too many illustrations than too few.

FAST APP

Consider an upcoming speech. Pick a concept or learning point that you'd love to bolster with a thought-provoking example or illustration. Then, set a timer for 10 minutes and see what you can come up with.

Go through your "Cool Things" and "Stories" files. Check your notes app or pocket notebook. Use the Internet. Ask a colleague. Do not censor anything. All ideas are good at this stage.

If you find one before the timer goes off, keep looking. Sometimes the one you find after searching for a while is the best.

Google Images is a trademark of Google Inc.

16

Handouts That Work

What we leave behind is a part of ourselves.
—Anatole France, winner of the
Nobel Prize in Literature 1921

You've just put the finishing touches on your speech (and it's not 2:00 A.M. the morning of the presentation.) Good for you. Now it's time to think about your handout or leave-behind.

The first question is: Does this presentation even need a handout? Often, handouts are complete afterthoughts that serve no real purpose. Before you spend time creating one, ask yourself why you're putting one together. Because everyone else does? Because you feel your presentation is not strong enough on its own? These are not good enough reasons, my friend.

The Purpose of a Handout

An effective leave-behind serves one of three functions:

1. It helps the audience process information during the presentation.

2. It provides detail and supporting information you don't have time to cover.

3. It serves as a reference tool or job aid after the presentation.

If none of these functions apply to your presentation, a handout may not be needed.

Handout Dos and Don'ts

If you determine that a handout is a good idea, or if your boss or client requires one, here are some dos and don'ts for making it effective:

DO
*   Be concise. Shorter is better.
*   Use bulleted and numbered lists.
*   Highlight key information with boldface, italics, underlining, or colored text.
*   Allow plenty of white space for readability.
*   Provide adequate space for attendees to take notes.
*   Put heavy data and research in an appendix at the back of the handout.
*   Consider making it interactive (see below).

DON'T
*   Send your handout to people ahead of time. (Only a small percentage will read it in advance, and then you're challenged with informed and uninformed sub-groups within your overall audience.)

- Associate quantity with quality.
- Include so much information that your audience is tempted to read the handout instead of paying attention to you.
- Use more than two fonts throughout the entire handout.
- Place the chart or graph caption above the chart or graph. People are used to finding it below.
- Forget to include your contact information.
- Simply print out your PowerPoint slide deck as your handout (more on this, below).

Consider Making It Interactive

An interactive handout is one that requires active participation by your audience. Key parts of the handout are intentionally left blank, requiring participants to listen more carefully and encouraging them to take additional notes. Such handouts can feature fill-in-the-blanks, graph or picture labeling, a structured outline with room for notes, etc.

The advantage of interactive handouts is that they convert your audience from being passive listeners to active participants. Their use not only increases the effectiveness of your presentation through deepened audience engagement, it also increases your audience's enjoyment and creates a greater feeling of collaboration in the room.

Of course, interactive handouts are not appropriate for every presentation you make. But when they are (e.g., in training sessions, sales presentations, or continuing education classes), they can be particularly effective tools.

Breaking out of
Printed-Slide-Deck-As-Handout Prison

Don't make the mistake that 99% of American businesspeople do and simply print your PowerPoint slides as a handout. Here are seven reasons why:

1. A printed deck makes you, the speaker, irrelevant. (See Chapter 10.)
2. People tend to read ahead to get to the "good parts," so they stop listening to you.
3. You lose the opportunity to build anticipation or show the audience something they're not expecting.
4. Audience members rarely refer to the PowerPoint deck *after* the presentation, so why give them one?
5. If your audience needs handout materials during the presentation, a PowerPoint printout is rarely the right kind of information.
6. It's what every other presenter does, so your leave-behind won't stand out.
7. A printed deck is usually quite voluminous. It's wasteful and a drag on the environment.

Instead:
- Consider not having a printed handout. What? Yes, in an effort to be green, post the handout to your company's intranet or website, or send it to your audience electronically. Those who really want to can print it out for themselves.
- Don't print out your slides, but tell the audience they can have a "completed" deck (a set of your slides with the details filled in) after the presentation, if interested.

- If you <u>must</u> provide a copy of your deck, create your PowerPoint following the 4x4 Principle for text slides and using as many visuals as possible. (See Chapter 11.) Print it and hand it out. Even if your audience flips ahead, they will still need your input to fully comprehend the details behind your slides.
- Cut and paste the text of your slides into a Word document. The same information will take on a different feel when offered in a different format. Plus, I've found that audiences rarely read ahead in a Word document the way they do with a slide deck. I'm not exactly sure why, but I think it's the square boxes of the slides that make people think they're reading a comic strip or a storyboard. Trust me, Word is the way to go for handouts.

Another benefit of not giving your audience an exact copy of your slides kicks in on those rare occasions when your speaking time is unexpectedly cut short. If your listeners don't have a printed copy of what your slideshow was supposed to include, you are free to skip some slides without the audience knowing what they're missing. (For more on this technique, see Chapter 22.)

When Should You Distribute Your Handout?

You can adjust the impact of a leave-behind by choosing *when* to hand it out—at the start of your presentation, during the presentation, or as participants walk out the door. There's no right or wrong here. It's just a matter of what your audience needs to digest your information and act on it.

One creative solution is to distribute your handout page-by-page or section-by-section as your speech unfolds. One of my clients, a salesman, was frustrated that customers were reading his handout and flipping ahead to the "pricing section" instead of listening to him. So he decided to hand it out one section at a time as he came to each part of his presentation. Besides preventing his customers from reading ahead, it added freshness and a "this just in" news quality to his talk. The result? No one complained, he kept his audience engaged, and more importantly, he sold more.

If your handout is just an afterthought, your audience will regard it as such. However, if it has a purpose and you give it a little think time, you can use it to your advantage.

FAST APP

When crafting your next handout, ask yourself these questions and answer them with your specific presentation and audience in mind:

1. *What purpose will a handout serve for this speech?*
2. *How can I create a handout that makes me a more effective speaker?*
3. *How can my handout help the audience pay more attention to my points when I'm trying to make them?*
4. *Should I give it out at the beginning? During? At the end? Post it electronically?*

PART THREE:
DELIVERING YOUR SPEECH

17

The #1 Trust-Builder: Eye-to-Eye Contact

Your eyes tell the story before your mouth does.
—Michael Caine, Academy Award-winning actor

Have you ever attended a concert, play, or some other live performance where the performer delivered a line, stanza, or part of the chorus directly to you? Even if you were seated in an audience of hundreds or thousands, there was a shared moment between you and the person on stage in which you felt like you were the only person in the hall. Not to be too much like Dr. Phil, but how did that make you feel? I'm guessing you felt recognized, energized, and connected.

Wouldn't it be great to recreate that experience with your audience members every time you give a presentation? You can. That's what this chapter is all about.

In order for the audience (specifically, the key decision makers) to adopt your proposal, award you a contract, or consider a contrarian position, they need to believe in you. In addition to great content, the best way to accomplish this is to speak to individuals in the audience, looking them directly in the eye when you talk.

Presentation experts often talk about making good eye contact. That's great. But what exactly does that mean? How do you quantify that? And where's the line between good eye contact and a restraining order?

Eye contact tells us a lot about people. Whether you're interviewing a job candidate, meeting someone new at a conference, or going out on a first date, if the other person doesn't make sufficient and appropriate eye contact, you begin to make all sorts of assumptions. Is he not interested? Lacking in confidence? Hiding something? Running from the law? Any way you slice it, it isn't good.

People's perceptions about eye contact have been tested in scores of studies. According to one study[1], the ideal amount of eye contact during one-on-one encounters is between 45-60% of the time. As long as the speaker doesn't stare, more than 60% is perfectly permissible. Dipping below 45% generates a poor rating from the other person on a variety of criteria—attractiveness, credibility, and the ability to connect.

Now let's take this information into a presentation room. The audience, whether a group of 20, 200, or 2,000, is made up of individuals, and the presenter needs to connect with each one of them during her speech. (Really? Yes. More on connecting with large crowds later in this chapter.) However, most speakers regard the audience as a general group and try to look at everyone all at once, with their eyes scanning back and forth across the crowd. A far superior approach is to speak to individuals one at a time, as though each is the only person in the room. A great presentation, then, is made up of a series of these one-on-one mini-conversations. Each audience member feels acknowledged and validated.

The key to creating these one-on-one connections is Eye-to-Eye Contact.

Eye-to-Eye Contact: How It Works

Eye-to-Eye Contact is a simple, three-step process:

1. Lock eyes with one member of your audience.
2. Deliver a complete thought while looking at that one person.
3. Then, insert a brief pause into your speech while you look for the next person to address. (Be sure your pause is silent. No "um"s.)

Then, simply repeat the process.

How long should you speak to one person? Just long enough to make a short point—usually a sentence or two. Common markers indicating it's time to move on to someone else are when you need to take a breath or at a natural pause in your line of thought.

How long is the pause between people? This is more art than science and can range between a nanosecond and a second or two. It really depends. (See Chapter 19 for more on pauses.) The speech should still be delivered in a smooth, conversational manner, not a halting staccato.

The Benefits of Eye-to-Eye Contact

Here are the key benefits of this approach:

- *It shrinks the room.*
  Engaging individual members of the audience, in effect, shrinks the audience from a lot of people down to just one.

Among other things, this reduces stress for the presenter. It's easy to talk to one person, right?

- ***It lets the speaker read the audience.***
  Each time you lock onto someone's eyes, you get a quick snapshot of how they're doing. Are they smiling and nodding their head? Nodding off? Taking notes? Daydreaming? Looking flustered? As you take a continuous pulse of your audience, you can adjust your delivery, as needed.

- ***It conveys confidence and builds trust.***
  From a body language perspective, nothing enhances faith in the speaker's message better than taking the time to look each listener in the eye. Add in a balanced stance and open-palm gestures and you're a one-person trust-building machine. (More on gestures in Chapter 18.)

- ***It slows you down.***
  By taking brief pauses between people, Eye-to-Eye Contact helps regulate the pace of your speech and prevents you from talking faster than your audience can handle.

- ***It compels people to listen.***
  Even if the person you're speaking to isn't looking directly back at you, he still knows he's being spoken to. Remember in high school when you knew the teacher was talking right at you while you were looking down at your desk? Eye-to-Eye Contact is a way of holding audience members accountable (in a good way), as if you're saying, "Hey, I'm looking at you. Pay attention." It makes it

considerably more difficult for people to check email on their cell phones.

That's all the good stuff.   But the idea of making eye contact with individual audience members tends to raise questions. Following are the four most common.

FAQ about Eye-to-Eye Contact

Q: *Won't people feel ill at ease if I "call them out" visually?*
A: Yes and no. They will definitely feel uncomfortable if you stare at them too long. That's why Eye-to-Eye Contact lasts only as long as it takes to deliver a single thought. Think in terms of seconds, not tens of seconds. As long as you don't stare, they'll feel included and not ill at ease.

Q: *I feel uncomfortable looking people in the eye while I'm speaking.*
A: (Technically this is a statement, not a question, but I'll answer it anyway—with a question.) Do you look people in the eye when you are talking one-on-one or in a small meeting? I'm guessing the answer is "yes." So why not do the same in more formal presentations? This question usually comes up because the questioner tends to be looking at individual audience members too long. One thought is long enough.

Q: *How is this supposed to work with a large audience of, say, more than 100 people?*
A: Eye-to-Eye Contact works as well with large audiences as it does with small ones. Imagine yourself standing before 200 people in a hotel meeting room (scary as that may seem).

Envision picking out and focusing on the person in the third-to-last row, six seats in from the left. Thanks to perceived angles and lines of sight, the four to six people immediately around this person can't help but think you're looking at them and them alone. So, you're actually able to connect with more people more quickly. Trust me, it works.

Q: *What if I'm addressing a group from another culture, in which looking people directly in the eye isn't socially acceptable?*
A: By all means, please adjust your delivery to meet the audience's needs and norms. Cultural sensitivity to eye contact is an important aspect of audience analysis. (See Chapter 4.)

Among all the presentation skills, Eye-to-Eye Contact is by far the most valuable for developing the audience's trust in you. They may not be able to put their finger on why, but they will feel a great connection to you and your material. All else being equal, you'll be amazed how much more weight people give your arguments when you look them in the eye.

FAST APP

Do an experiment. When you're out at lunch with co-workers or friends, or in a meeting with three or more people, decide that you'll speak only when you're looking someone in the eye—not while you're gazing out the window or even catching the waiter's attention. Connect eye-to-eye with one person, say a complete thought to her, and then pause briefly (in silence) while you choose the next person to talk to.

At first, don't try to maintain Eye-to-Eye Contact throughout an entire gathering (as your head might explode and that would really put a damper on lunch). Start with 30 seconds and then slowly work your way up until this becomes your default speaking style. Rest assured, you will be amazed at the positive reaction you get from this technique.

18

Killer Delivery Skills

*Always be a first-rate version of yourself instead of
a second-rate version of somebody else.*
—Judy Garland, legendary
award-winning singer and actress

**If you were to survey books about presentation
skills** or look at the course descriptions for a public speaking
class, you would see considerable ink (words, not tattoos)
devoted to the ways in which speakers are "supposed" to
physically deliver a speech In other words, how they are
supposed to stand, what to do with their hands, how much they
should walk around, etc. In reality, there is no "right" way. The
best way to deliver a presentation is in your own unique style
(cue "Kumbaya"). Your goal is to eliminate any distracting
habits so the audience can focus solely on your message. To
illustrate this, let's take a look at Hollywood.

Moviegoers are likely to forgive the lower production
values of a movie if the film has a good plot, strong characters,
solid acting, and a well-written script. However, most people
feel ripped-off if they throw down $12 to see the latest
blockbuster that has cutting-edge special effects and incredible
action sequences, but a predictable, boring story or uninspired
characters. The same is true for presentations: People crave
substance over flash.

Or, content trumps delivery.

That said, physical delivery skills are still important. So where do we start? As Judy Garland pointed out, if you try to give a presentation in any speaking style other than your own, you will come across as inauthentic. In case you didn't know, when it comes to effective presentations, authenticity reigns supreme.

The best way to develop great delivery skills is not to force yourself into a particular style, but rather to *free yourself* from any habits or mannerisms that distract the audience from hearing your message. These usually have to do with:

- How you stand
- What you do with your hands
- How loudly you speak
- How fast you speak

Other components like facial expressions, timing, and vocal inflection will take care of themselves once you master these four main elements. Here's what works and why.

Get Out of the Phone Booth:
Stance and Movement

The quickest way to look nervous and unnatural is to lock yourself in an imaginary phone booth—feet nailed to the floor, rarely venturing out, with very little use of the stage, and understated hand gestures close to the torso. Very boring. (For those of you who never knew life without a cell phone, phone booths are those small glass boxes on the streets of Metropolis where Clark Kent transforms himself into Superman.) Most presenters get stuck in the phone booth because just about every other speaker they've seen presents that way and they don't want to look stupid. "Play it safe" is their mantra.

Before we talk about good stage movement, we need to identify what makes a good stance. A good, confident stance is one in which your weight is evenly distributed on each leg and your feet are about shoulder-width apart. Confidence and strength are associated with balance, and people find this more credible than tilting to one side with most of your weight on one leg. As long as you are balanced, it doesn't matter exactly how your feet are positioned on the floor—splayed out, pigeon-toed, etc. Just whatever feels comfortable. That's your call.

Now, if you're feeling a bit adventurous, it's time to step out of that phone booth. You see, the nervous energy that builds naturally when we speak needs an outlet. Otherwise, it will come out in ways you won't like. A great way to release nervous (i.e., pent up) energy is to take a few steps from time to time during your speech. Take two or three steps to your right, left, front, or even back and then plant your feet in a balanced position, and make a point or two. Repeat as needed. The audience will appreciate your purposeful movement and the change of pace. And as energy is released through your legs, the rest of your body is freed up to express itself more naturally.

Show and Tell:
Gestures That Enhance Your Message

Another way to reduce nervous energy and get out of the phone booth is to make gestures out and away from your torso with your hands. Gestures help bring the content of your speech to life in a way that is visually appealing. Think about how gestures enhance what a frustrated parent is saying to a toddler at a grocery store. If she says, "I've had it up to here!" her hand flies up to the top of her forehead. It would look a little ridiculous if she left her hand at her side. The child needs a visual cue to know how much more patience remains before mom starts dishing out the punishment. Your presentation is no different. Give your audience as much visual stimulation as you can to keep them dialed in and attentive.

Consider, for instance, when talking about numbers how easy and natural it is to do the following: Indicate an increase (raise your hand up), a decrease (do the opposite), a plateau (both hands making the "safe" sign in baseball), uneven results...(you get the idea). Or, if talking about time, you might point to the right to connote the past and to the left for the future (because that's how your audience views a timeline from their perspective, not yours). Of course, these are examples of things you *can* do, not necessarily movements you're "supposed" to do. Remember to stick with what's natural for you.

Another instinctive way we use expressive gestures is when presenting a comparison—old vs. new, A or B, two competitors, etc. Move both hands to the right side of your body when talking about one and then indicate the other on your left. Again, my descriptions are just to give you an idea of movement, not necessarily recommendations. You'll have your own natural way of expressing yourself. During my presentation skills workshops, it's amazing to see a dozen people express the same idea with their hands in 12 distinct ways. Just be yourself and let it flow.

For other ideas, think how you use body language when someone is at a distance and can't hear your voice. It forces you to communicate more creatively. Or, watch how people use body language when they don't speak the same language. Gestures become essential and, by necessity, more effective.

Vocal Inflection: The Beneficiary of Good Gestures

As you practice using expressive gestures while speaking, you will find that your voice's inflection (and volume) will improve at the same time. Almost without exception, when people extend their arms and gesture from their shoulders away from their torso, their voices register a temporary volume increase and their inflection goes up. So be dramatic with your gestures and you will find that your voice will have more texture and vocal variety, even during conference calls.

An excellent way to improve your vocal inflection is to read children's books aloud (preferably to a child). Give each character a different voice. Make an effort to bring the story to life and paint a vivid picture of the scene in the child's mind. Do this, and you'll naturally bring more vocal dimension to your next talk.

Want to scare yourself silly? Call yourself from another phone and listen to your voicemail greeting. Did it sound like your dog just died? If you were a client or prospect, would listening to your voice ruin an otherwise good day? How much inflection did you hear? Did you sound engaging, winsome, and upbeat or more like you're about to be audited? Now, re-record your voicemail greeting, but this time do these three things: stand up, smile, and gesture freely as if the person calling you were actually in the room. Chances are you'll sound more energetic, conversational, friendly, and engaging. You can apply the same approach to your face-to-face talks.

Turn It Up: Good Volume

Regardless of the size and shape of the room, a presenter should speak at a volume slightly higher than normal conversational level. A nice, strong voice says: "Hey, audience, listen to me. This is important. I believe in what I'm saying and you should, too."

If you are not sure of the proper volume to use in a particular room, do a sound check. Before your speech, ask a colleague to sit near the back of the room and let you know how loudly you're coming across. Also have him give you periodic volume checks with hand signals during your presentation. Take note of any background noise like air conditioning, traffic outside the window, conversations in the hallway, and even people talking in the back of the room. When in doubt, too loud is better than too soft.

Good Pace: Finding the Right Speed

The optimal rate of speech differs for each speaker. In brief, the ideal pace is fast enough to keep people interested, but not so fast that they are confused. Think about everyday conversations. Both a fast talker and "Mr. Molasses" can be off-putting. Strive for the middle ground.

Surging adrenaline when you're making a presentation will naturally increase your pace. Plus, speakers often start speaking quickly because they're nervous and just want to get the presentation over with as quickly as possible. Similar to getting feedback on volume, enlist a colleague to give you subtle signals about your pace—speed up, slow down, don't change (and even the "A-OK" sign to tell you you're looking good).

Also, during your speech, don't be afraid to vary your speed based on what you're trying to convey. A slightly quicker pace connotes importance while a slower rate allows audience members to absorb key points.

Self-Perception Doesn't Equal Reality

We've all heard that perception is reality—i.e., that what people perceive to be real might as well be real. However, things get a little distorted when it comes to self-perception, especially for speakers.

Most presenters perceive themselves as:

- Speaking louder than they actually do.
- Talking slower than they really do.
- Making gestures that are larger and more expressive than they truly are.
- Making more eye contact with the audience than they really do.
- Having more range and inflection in their voice than they actually do.

In other words, you can probably double your volume, exaggerate your gestures, and move around a lot more than feels comfortable, and you'll look and sound just right to your audience. Or, to put it another way, just get out of the phone booth and you'll do fine.

Presenting Slides with Flair:
The G.E.T. System

Presenting PowerPoint slides like a rock star starts with having more images and fewer words on your slides (see Chapter 11). Fewer words frees you up to connect better with your audience and be more conversational because you'll spend more time facing them instead of looking at the screen. (I'm no dating expert, but you typically don't see people on first dates with their backs to each other. Not a good recipe for building rapport.) Remember, your audience is going to read your slides out of natural curiosity anyway, so why not help them along as they digest your material?

A great way to present slides is to use the G.E.T. System:

1. *Glance* briefly at the screen or your laptop to get an idea of what you are going say about the current slide being shown (in silence. No "um"s).

2. *Engage* the audience by turning to face them or looking up at them.

3. *Tell* the audience what they're looking at.

With 4x4 slides, try to deliver one bullet point to one person. With slides that have a lot of text, just discuss the slide's topic in general terms. WARNING: Do NOT read text-heavy slides word-for-word. The only exceptions to this ironclad, carved-in-stone rule are when you're discussing a mission statement, citing a specific statute, or reviewing testimony in which the exact wording is absolutely critical.

Another way to think about presenting PowerPoint slides is to view each slide as a "mini agenda" of what you're going to say over the next few minutes. Briefly give an overview of the entire slide, mentioning a bit about each bullet point, then go over the main points in more detail.

The Best Place to Stand

Given the fact that conference rooms, boardrooms, meeting rooms, and courtrooms vary greatly, where is the optimal place to position yourself while delivering slides? I recommend you imitate Vanna White of "Wheel of Fortune" fame. Typically, she stands just to one side of the word puzzle and slightly in front of it. You can do the same in relation to the screen. As you reveal a new slide, try to stand a few feet in front of the screen and just to the left of it from the audience's point of view. Why the left? Because, in the Western Hemisphere, we read from left to right and this makes it easier on the audience. From this vantage point, you can easily see both the screen and the audience without turning your back on them when you glance at the screen. Plus, you're not likely to block anyone's view. After you give a quick overview of the slide, feel free to step closer to the audience or to move wherever you'd like.

The following **FAST APP** offers options to practice your stance and gestures that will take about five minutes each. The goal is for these skills to become so natural to you that, when you stand up to present in front of a group, it will feel no different than normal.

FAST APP

The following are just a few ideas for practicing killer delivery skills in quick bursts throughout your busy day.

STANCE

Make a deal with yourself that at least once a day, you will strike the "presenter's pose" (your feet shoulder-width apart and your weight spread evenly across both feet). Notice how it feels to stand this way. Get comfortable with it. Soon, you will begin to feel more comfortable standing like this in front of a group. Where can you work on your stance? Anywhere you have to stand for a period of time. For instance:

- In the elevator (if you ride one at work each day—even if it's just to the 2nd floor)
- Waiting in line at Starbucks® or your local deli
- Brushing your teeth, applying make-up, shaving, or fixing dinner (Hopefully you're not doing all these things at the same time.)

GESTURES

When you're talking to someone on the phone, use speakerphone or a headset and work on your gestures. In addition to being good practice for you, you might be surprised at the reaction you get from the person on the other end of the phone.

For a great example of people gesturing effectively when no one can see them, check out the vocal recording sessions in the DVD bonus features of any animated film. The actors use wild and dramatic gestures so that their voices (and characters) come to life on screen. It's almost impossible to sound engaging and winsome with your arms "strapped" to your sides.

Starbucks is a registered trademark of Starbucks Corporation.

19

Pause:
The Power of Silence

You never saw a fish on a wall with its mouth shut.
—Sally Berger, writer and new media curator

Have you ever fallen asleep watching TV? (C'mon, admit it. Happens to everybody.) Then, if the TV signal temporarily goes out, or there's a brief gap between commercials, suddenly that silence rouses you from your slumber like a 6:00 A.M. alarm clock buzzer. How peculiar that the absence of sound awakens you so forcefully.

The same applies in presentations. As awesome as any speaker's voice quality might be, after a while it can start to sound monotonous. However, you have a powerful tool in your arsenal that can be used strategically throughout your speech to great effect: The pause.

The Benefits of a Well-Timed Pause

A well-timed pause accomplishes several things. For starters, it lets the presenter collect his thoughts. It gives you an opportunity to formulate what you want to say next, which can greatly reduce your verbal gymnastics (e.g., when you start a sentence poorly and then have to do all sorts of grammatical gyrations to finish the thought coherently).

A pause also allows your audience a few seconds to process what you just said, flip to the next page in the handout, or even jot down some notes. This is critical, especially if you're delivering complex data or are discussing a controversial topic and you're trying to change people's minds. As much as you and your listeners may love the sound of your voice, brief respites of silence are like cups of cool, refreshing water for a thirsty audience.

The Length of a Pause

How long should a pause be? It depends. But generally, a good pause is several seconds long. Be warned: A two- or three-second pause will seem like an eternity to you while you're giving a talk because speakers abhor silence, but it will sound like heaven to your audience. Even nanosecond pauses are welcome.

Caution: A Pause in a Presentation Should be Silent

Note that the title of this chapter is "Pause: The Power of Silence." Yes, a pause in a presentation should be silent. "What other kind of pause is there?" you may wonder. The truth is, presenters make many pauses that aren't silent at all.

For instance, many speakers pause when they need to think or look at their notes. But instead of a brief moment of silence, they use all kinds of unwelcome utterances like "um," "uh," and "you know." These verbal tics are like static on the radio. They make it hard for people to concentrate on the main content of the presentation.

Another way people audibly pause is when using a "thinking phrase"— a word or string of words that buys them a few seconds as they consider what to say next. This phrase may work great and flow well with the presentation at first. However, for some presenters, use of such a phrase as a "verbal pause" can become a bad habit. They may unknowingly repeat such a phrase too often, causing it to become as annoying as "um" and "uh." A few examples:

- I once attended a conference in which the emcee tended to use the phrase, "and things of that nature" at the end of sentences in which he was listing items. After a while, the audience couldn't help but laugh. During his pre-lunch instructions, he said, "Down the hall and to the right you'll find the bathrooms and things of that nature." Huh?

- In a presentation to prospective students at a well-known university, an admissions office representative kept ending her descriptions of the school's selling points with "etcetera, etcetera, etcetera." This wasn't especially helpful in giving the students and parents in attendance a clear picture of the school's offerings. "We have seven schools: The College of Arts & Sciences, the School of Engineering, the School of Nursing, etcetera, etcetera, etcetera."

- A department head at a leading manufacturing company fell into the habit of using the word "fundamentally" all the time. Now, when you use a word like "fundamentally," it should be followed by a bedrock principle or something of core importance. However, this gentleman used the word so often that it bled not only into his presentations, but also into his everyday speech. "Fundamentally, we need better snacks in the break room."

Incorporating Pauses into Your Presentation

Here are three ways to incorporate effective pauses into your presentation:

1. **"P" is for Pause**

    Look over your speech outline or written presentation when it's completed and take a few minutes to determine the places where you would like the audience to reflect on a particular point. At each of these points on your outline, write a large "P" in bright ink and circle it. Then, during your presentation, when you see the "P," force yourself to pause.

2. **Ask a Question**

    Similar to jotting down "P"s, look for places to pose a question and mark them with a "Q." Even if you don't want the audience to answer out loud, asking a rhetorical question will dial them in. While they're thinking, you have a natural moment to pause and catch your breath.

    In lieu of a question, you can offer a thought-provoking statement. For example, if you're recommending to the COO of your company that you switch vendors, you could say, "Any outside auditor would tell us we're crazy if we stick with our current vendor." Then, let him ruminate about the impact of your suggestion for a few seconds.

3. **"W" for is for Walk**

When using PowerPoint, a natural place to pause and let your audience mull over a thought is when you glance down or walk over to your laptop to advance your presentation to the next slide. Mentally mark these points with a "W." There's an instinctive impulse to continue talking. But if you give into it, many of your words will be spoken to the floor or your computer screen and not to your audience. Why not walk over to your laptop in a natural moment of silence? Your listeners will get a break and you'll give yourself a chance to think about what you want to say next. While it's not necessary to do so, at times you can introduce this period of silence by saying something as simple as, "Let's go to the next slide." Then, as you stroll the two to three steps to your laptop, the quietness will seem natural and welcome.

To Click or Not to Click?

Human beings have struggled for eons (okay, for 30 years) with the question of whether or not to use a hand-held remote control (a.k.a. a "clicker") to advance their PowerPoint slides. Unless the layout of the room precludes it, I recommend not using a remote (in the traditional sense) for two reasons:

1. Most speakers who hold onto a clicker inadvertently begin to fiddle with it after a while, tossing it casually from hand to hand, tapping on it, or spinning it on their palm. This is

an unnecessary distraction. Plus, it is all too easy to accidentally hit a button and advance to the next slide before you're ready. Clumsy? Yes. Professional? No.

2. The opposite may occur. Instead of playing with it, the speaker may immobilize the arm that's holding it, reducing gestures to understated, phone booth lameness.

If you *must* have a remote or your laptop is too far from where you stand, here's a thought: Put it down on a nearby table or on the podium. You don't need to hold it for the 95% of the time it is not in use. That way, you're free to gesture at will, and you can get to the remote when you need it.

FAST APP

Take a look at your next presentation. Spend several minutes identifying at least five places where you can write a big red "P" for a pause, a "Q" to prompt a question, or a mental "W" to remind you to take a quiet walk to your laptop (or to the remote that you smartly put down on a table).

20

Managing Today's Shrinking Attention Span

He has the attention span of a lightning bolt.
[The same goes for most audiences.]
— Robert Redford, iconic actor and director

Pop Quiz: (Don't worry, this won't count toward your final grade.) How long is the average attention span of a live audience?

> 15 minutes?
> A half hour?
> An hour?
> As long as there's coffee?

You might want to sit down for this. According to *The Trainer's Pocketbook*[1], it's as short as 10 minutes! This means that, if the presenter does not actively engage the audience's attention, they are likely to tune you out in the time it takes to microwave a couple of Hot Pockets®.

In a 30-minute speech, the audience could mentally "check out" three-plus times. Even when your audience is genuinely interested in the topic, scores of other concerns can tug at their attention: an unresolved customer issue, the thought of urgent emails piling up in their inbox, the big playoff game that day, perhaps a sick loved one at home. Take your pick.

Here are some easy-to-execute attention-grabbing tactics that you can incorporate into your next presentation. Try to use one of them every eight to ten minutes.

Shift yourself physically.
* Walk to different place in the room or on the dais.
* If you're sitting, find a reason to stand up—perhaps to write something on a flip chart.
* When presenting from behind a podium, step out to one side to drive home an important point.

Shift the audience's focus.
* Use a quote (humorous or thought-provoking) to reinforce an idea.
* Tell a brief story that's relevant to the topic at hand.
* Blank out the PowerPoint slide with the "B" or "W" key (then, hitting any key will bring the slide back).
* Switch visual media. Go from PowerPoint to a flip chart or a prop.
* Share the microphone. Ask a colleague to discuss a point on which she has expertise. (Arrange this ahead of time so that there are no surprises.)
* Show a one-panel cartoon to illuminate a particular point.

Shift what the audience is doing.
* Give your audience a break. —Not necessarily every 10 minutes, but from time to time, you might consider a two-minute-stay-in-the-room-stand-up-break. (Yes, that's the official name.)

- Ask a rhetorical question. Mentally put the ball in their court.
- Have a mini Q&A session—nothing formal, just a way to get them talking and give feedback.
- Encourage them to text you a question, comment, or concern. (You'll see who it's from, but you can share the information anonymously).
- Break the audience up into small groups for a quick activity to discuss a point or brainstorm how to apply the information you're providing.
- Create a "forced debate." Assign different sides of an issue to two people or two groups of people and ask them to argue their position for a few minutes.

Attention span tactics don't have to be elaborate; they just need to be well-executed. And well-timed.

FAST APP

How long is your next presentation? Divide the number of minutes by 10 to determine how often your audience will most likely space out on you. What will you do to reset your audience's attention span clock? Draw from the list above or come up with an idea of your own.

Hot Pockets is a registered trademark of Société des Produits Nestlé S.A.
(Incidentally, my wife thought I couldn't work Hot Pockets into this book. I've now proven her wrong. Sorry, Honey.)

21

Give 'Em the Gift of Time

Be wise in the use of time. The question in life is not 'how much time do we have?' The question is 'what shall we do with it?'
—Anna Robertson Brown Lindsay,
first woman to earn a doctorate
at the University of Pennsylvania

What is the most valuable commodity on the planet? Precious metals? Six-pack abs? Your fully-charged cell phone? None of the above. The most precious commodity is time.

Time pressures today are so great that Leslie Perlow, the Konosuke Matsushita Professor of Leadership at Harvard Business School, suggests that corporate America today suffers from a "time famine."[1] Our "busyness" is not confined to the workplace, however. According to a study cited on Time.com[2] (no pun intended), 58% of Americans would pay $2,725 in cold, hard cash "to have an extra hour in their over-crowded day." We are as busy as ever and spare time is hard to come by.

If everyone is completely starved for time, why not give a little of it back to your audience during your next presentation? They'll love you for it.

Consider the standard scenario in which you're asked to give a presentation at work. Once you know the topic, you next need to know how long you have to speak. 30 minutes? An hour? Two hours? Good question.

Here's where many people make a mistake. They assume that they *have* to speak for the entire designated time, whether they need the full amount or not. I think this goes back to writing assignments in middle school, where students sometimes focus more on hammering out the required number of words than on delivering quality content. In truth, an audience is far more interested in hearing a compelling message than making sure you fill up the entire time slot.

When considering the length of your speech, ask yourself these two questions:

1. How much time do I really need to establish and prove my point(s)?
2. If I were sitting in the audience, how much of my time would I be willing to invest in hearing about this topic?

Brief Is the New Black

If you're given an hour, but you can effectively accomplish your goal in 45 minutes, why not give the gift of 15 minutes back to your audience? Brevity is not just about time, it can also make your presentation more effective. In fact, some of history's greatest speeches were surprisingly short (yet memorable):

- Lincoln's Gettysburg Address: 2 minutes (just 272 words)
- FDR's Pearl Harbor "infamy" speech: 7 minutes
- Martin Luther King, Jr.'s "I Have a Dream" speech: 16 minutes

Let brevity carry the day. This applies especially to the dreaded Presentation Dead Zones: Right after lunch and at the end of the day. Regardless of how fantastic the speaker is, as the clock ticks closer to the end of the scheduled time, listeners' interest and attention have left the building.

Now, I'm not suggesting that you deliver a 2-minute Gettysburg Address if you've been given a 60-minute time slot for your speech. I would not cut down more than 25% of your speaking time or your client or boss might get upset. And it's, of course, vital that you in no way shortchange the essential message of your presentation. The key here is to recognize that there is no rule that you have to use every minute of the time you've been given to speak. Rather, let the goals of your presentation be the driver. If you can accomplish them in a shorter amount of time, your delivery will be more to-the-point and your audience will appreciate the margin.

On Running Long

A corollary to giving the gift of time is to make sure you never, ever go over your allotted amount of time. This does not go over well with audiences and may throw an organization's agenda off for the rest of the day. In fact, it's yet another reason to plan on not using the maximum amount of time you've been given. This will help you stay within your time parameter even if you have an especially robust Q&A session or if your client starts your portion of the meeting late (as can definitely happen).

Be prepared: If you do finish your speech early, people may come up and kiss you. Some of them might even name their kids after you. Or, at the very least, they'll thank you for it.

FAST APP

After crafting your next presentation, take a good hard look to see if you can give some time back to your audience. Are you "over making" any of your points? Addressing anything that doesn't relate directly to your Take-Home Message? Even cutting two minutes off of a 15-minute presentation will make you a hero. And everybody loves a hero.

For more insights and examples of giving your audience more than they expect, visit www.HitYourStride.com.

22

Making Your Speech a Conversation

When you're talking, they're judging.
When they're talking, they're buying.
—Ketchum Advertising catchphrase

As an audience member waiting for a presentation to begin, wouldn't it be great to have direct input on the presentation content so that the speaker covers exactly what you want to hear about—nothing more and nothing less? That's what your audience *is* thinking every time you get up to speak. (Well, that and "Wow me.")

The best way to insure that you give them precisely what they really want is by asking them. What's on their minds? What are their hot buttons? What's keeping them up at night? How can you and your presentation help them?

But how do you deliver the information if you're asking questions and the audience is talking? You present your material in response to what they tell you when they answer your questions. In this way, the speech takes the form of a dialogue.

A dialogue between speaker and audience is more inclusive, more productive, and more kinetic than the standard speech. Yawns will become a thing of the past.

Why? Because every person's favorite topic in the whole world is himself/herself. Let's face it. No matter what your level of self-esteem is, we are 100% head-over-heels in love with ourselves. —We love our opinions, our clothes, our food, our politics, etc. We're ga-ga about "me." So why not let everyone's favorite person share the stage with you (metaphorically)?

A few years ago, I was tasked with helping a senior-level director at a national consulting firm improve his sales presentation. He was often getting to the final stage in the Request for Proposal ("RFP") process, but was having difficulty closing the sale in the final pitch meeting. I asked him to tell me when in his sales presentations his prospects have seemed the most engaged, as he should be looking to capitalize on those moments of great attentiveness. He said, "That's easy. It's when the prospect is talking about his own business." He paused and continued, "Come to think of it, they're not all that engaged when I'm talking about their business and they're almost comatose when I'm running through our firm's spiel." So, we set about making his sales pitch more conversational with the prospect being the star of the show.

Simply put, the more the audience talks, the better you look. Not a bad way to give a presentation.

Starting the Conversation

For the conversational speech format to work, you have to really know your stuff. You must be prepared to cover subjects out of order. And you must be willing to risk not being able to cover every single thing you had planned. Yet the result will be an audience that feels every minute was worthwhile and focused on them. And they'll be more inclined to buy from you or agree with you.

The key to giving a conversational talk is to ask customized, open-ended questions—that is, questions about the issues your audience is facing that cannot be answered with a simple "yes" or "no." The more open-ended your questions, the better the conversation; the better the conversation, the better the presentation. And you'll certainly need to tailor the questions to fit with the information you're presenting.

Here are 10 good questions to get you thinking and your audience talking:

1. What, if anything, has changed since we last met/talked?
2. What are your thoughts on...?
3. What are you hearing from your customers/clients/partners...?
4. What's your biggest obstacle to...?
5. How well do you...?
6. Can you give me an example of...?
7. What can we do to...?
8. Where do you see growth coming from in the near/long-term...?
9. If you could change...?
10. Where are your competitors not doing a good job?

Other good conversation starters are:
- Tell me about...
- Could you describe...?

- What if...?
- When does...?
- How might you...?

Additional Tips

Here are a few additional suggestions to help make your conversational format work:

1. ***Don't give up.***

   The less your audience knows you personally, the less likely they are to speak up in the beginning. So ask questions early and often and don't be discouraged if at first they don't respond. As the presentation proceeds and they become more comfortable, they will open up.

   A case in point: I once gave an hour-long, after-dinner speech to a group of investment bankers in midtown Manhattan. I began by asking questions. Silence. I spoke for a while longer and asked more questions. More silence. But I kept giving them opportunities to talk and answer questions.

   Finally, 35 minutes into the hour, I asked a question that resonated with them. One person started talking. This spurred someone else to comment. And then another. Before I knew it, the group had launched into a lively conversation about the hot issues of the day that could have lasted for hours. All I had to do was shepherd the discussion to keep it focused. I was able to make my points, all while the audience felt like they were driving the presentation.

2. *Be nimble with PowerPoint.*

If you're using PowerPoint, be sure you know your slides and the approximate slide numbers well so you can jump around in your deck based on the conversation. (A hint from tech support: To go to a particular slide in your deck, enter the number of the slide you want to display and then press "Enter." For example, to jump to slide 17, type "1" then "7" then "Enter." Voila!) Feel free to have a printed deck with slide numbers on hand for your own quick reference.

3. *End on a high note.*

Make sure you manage the clock. And no matter what happens during your conversational presentation, allow time at the end for a clear and compelling Call-to-Action.

FAST APP

Create a "Great Questions/Conversation Starters" file on your computer. To populate it, start a running list of questions from various sources, such as:

- *An audience member during other presentations*
- *Your customers, clients, suppliers, partners, and colleagues in your daily work life*
- *The leaders in your industry*

PART FOUR:
POLISHING YOUR SKILLS

23

Rehearsals:
Getting It Right Before Going Live

The rehearsal is where it all happens.
—Wayne Rogers, actor on M*A*S*H

What do a Broadway actress, an NFL linebacker, and a world-class magician all have in common?
Nope, it's not their tax bracket. They rehearse. A lot. They understand that performing at the highest level requires hundreds of hours of rehearsing their craft.

For the presenter, it's next to impossible to excel without quality rehearsal. Put it this way: Can you name one thing in life you were really good at the first time you tried it? Speeches are no different.

So how in the world are you supposed to find time to rehearse a presentation when there's barely enough time to write it in the first place? As with any project that might seem daunting or too big to handle, the key to getting it done—especially if time is at a premium—is to break it up into smaller, more manageable pieces. This goes not only for the writing side of it, but also for rehearsals. You don't always have to rehearse your presentation all at once. The main thing is that you rehearse in some fashion.

How to Rehearse Your Presentation

Before discussing when to rehearse, let's focus on how to rehearse well. Here are five suggestions:

1. ***Rehearse out loud.*** There's a HUGE difference between "saying" the words of your speech silently in your head and saying them out loud. Practicing out loud is the best way to identify transitions or sections that don't flow well, something you don't want to suddenly discover during the actual presentation.

2. Unless you're unbelievably good looking, ***don't practice in front of a mirror.*** It's more distracting than it is helpful. To see how you come across while you're presenting, I've got three words for you: cell phone camera. Any smartphone today has adequate video capabilities for recording a presentation. Please check your vanity at the door. —Don't watch your video and pick yourself apart physically (that's what personal trainers are for). Just watch yourself in a detached, clinical manner, the way your audience will see you. Then think about what you'd like to keep, toss, or improve about your delivery.

3. Whenever possible, ***arrive early for your presentation and spend some time in the presentation room.*** Get comfortable with the view of the audience from the front of the room, the lighting, the position of your laptop, and the audience's seating arrangement. If time permits, go through your presentation out loud. Move around the space and picture the people who will be sitting there. Then, when

you deliver the presentation in front of the live audience, it will be your second time in that setting, and your comfort level will be much higher.

4. If you don't have access to the presentation room ahead of time, *try to find a space that closely approximates the actual room.* I typically rehearse in the basement of my house because it has the most open space and can feel like a meeting room.

5. *Don't forget Fido.* If you're dying for a real, live audience member with a pulse and brain waves, but you don't want to practice in front of a (human) loved one or co-worker, why not rehearse in front of your pet? Pets generally just sit and stare at you (hoping you have food) and their queries during Q&A are usually tame.

What to Rehearse When Time is Short

If, like most people, you're pressed for time and can't rehearse your whole speech, here are the three essential components you should rehearse before any presentation: the opening, the closing, and your transitions.

1. *Rehearsing the speech's opening should be at the top of your priority list.* Make sure you have the first few minutes of your speech down cold. It's during this period that your audience sizes you up and determines whether or not they will be favorably disposed toward you and your material— not to mention whether or not they should even pay attention to you.

2. *Next, rehearse the conclusion.* You don't want your speech to end with a fizzle. Know and be comfortable with your specific Call-to-Action. The last thing people hear is most likely the one thing they're going to remember. (Attention, page- and chapter-skippers: You can learn more about what makes a good Call-to-Action by checking out Chapter 5.)

3. *Finally, practice your transition from each main section to the next.* Most presenters spew forth the majority of their "um"s and "uh"s when they're searching for the best segue from one point to another. Practicing your transitions will eliminate these verbal annoyances.

If you happen to have time left after rehearsing your opening, closing, and transitions, rehearse your main points in a more in-depth manner.

When to Rehearse Your Presentation

In a perfect world, you would finish writing your speech a week or two before the actual presentation and then carve out plenty of time to practice. When you're able to do this, you'll find that that amount of advance preparation and practice will be to your great advantage. It's what all of us who give presentations should shoot for.

That being said, we don't live in a perfect world and you may often find yourself with less than optimal chunks of time in which to rehearse. Instead of insulting you with lists of ways in which you could make your days more productive in order to carve out speech rehearsal time ("Stop surfing the Internet." "Watch less TV!"—*Yes, we know.*), I'll simply say this: Rehearsing your speech is vitally important. Therefore, given the competing priorities of what I'm sure is a very busy schedule, you'll need to be creative in finding time to practice.

The following examples illustrate some creative ways in which your fellow speech-givers have carved out time to rehearse:

- A product manager at a global foods company used to practice her presentations in the shower. She liked the opportunity to rehearse out loud, away from the distractions of the day. Doing so allowed her to make sure her word choice flowed well, and it gave her the opportunity to anticipate questions and practice her Q&A. She's not the first person to report that some of her best thinking and problem solving occurs in the shower. What a great way to maximize the time you'd be spending there anyway.

- A flight attendant at Southwest Airlines once told me how difficult it is to pass the "FAA Public Announcement Test" required for work in his job. The information that needs to be relayed to the passengers is deemed so important that if you say a single word out of order or get even one syllable wrong, you fail the test. Since his busy schedule precluded him from practicing while actually in a plane, he would rehearse the various on-board announcements while driving his car. To tie his in-car rehearsals to on-plane moments (and to help him remember to rehearse), he would run through the pre-flight announcements whenever he fastened his seatbelt in the garage and he'd practice his arrival and crosscheck announcements whenever he parked at his destination. Nice.

- The development director of a non-profit shared that he practices his presentations while cutting the grass. He focuses on a specific part of his speech for about 8-10 rows of mowing, then shifts to a different section of his talk for the next 8-10 rows. Adopting this strategy has added significantly to his preparedness and confidence. And it has paid off. —His recent speeches have resulted in significantly increased donations (and he has a beautiful lawn).

Take a look at your schedule and figure out what works best for you. The main thing is that you rehearse. The more, the better. But some is better than none.

FAST APP

Think about the routine of your typical workweek (and weekend). Identify two places and times when you could rehearse your next presentation, whether it's during exercise, gardening, commuting...whatever. It's your call.

Then, try to rehearse your whole speech, substantial chunks or, at the very least, your opening, closing, and transitions during those two times.

24

"Be Prepared": Presentation Obstacles and Opportunities

A Scout must prepare himself by previously thinking out and practicing how to act in any accident or emergency so that he is never taken by surprise.
—Sir Robert Baden-Powell,
founder of the world scouting movement

Are you truly prepared for your speech? Really? Does this include having planned for an unexpected speaking emergency?

What if you showed up for a career-defining business presentation to a potential new client only to find that your main competitor had walked off with your presentation materials two minutes before the meeting? If you're thinking it could never happen, think again.

Back in my advertising days, my agency was one of four finalists for a plum medical association account. We're talking millions of dollars and lots of great exposure. The four finalists were invited to deliver their two-hour presentations back-to-back on the same day, with only a 15-minute break between each one. While one agency was presenting, the next would have their pitch team sitting in the lobby with all their stuff, ready to go.

During the commotion of the transition between two of the other finalists, the departing agency inadvertently got their presentation materials and portfolios mixed up with those of the agency on deck—and took *everything* with them out the door. (To be fair, all large, flat, black portfolio cases look alike.) The creative director for the ad agency about to present was in the bathroom while this was happening. He entered the boardroom with minutes to spare—only to discover that his team had no layouts, storyboards, or visual aids to show their prospective client. Yikes!

They quickly realized that all their hard work had just walked out of the building and was neatly situated in the trunk of their competitor's car, headed east on Interstate 70. And they had no backup plan. They had to improvise and "fill time" while they waited for the portfolios to be returned, which totally threw them off their game. Spoiler alert: They did not win the account. Go figure.

Don't let that happen to you.

I'm going to go out on a limb here and say that life is uncertain. (There, I said it.) Things happen that we don't expect or could never have anticipated. Smart speakers are ready to handle the obstacles that are thrown their way. Likewise, they're also ready to capitalize on the unexpected opportunities that sometimes arise on presentation day. They key is to be ready for the obstacles and open to the opportunities.

Before Your Speech:
The Value of a Backup Plan

Patricia Fripp, a member of the National Speakers Association Hall of Fame, once posed this question to an audience of consultants: "How good would you be if your PowerPoint didn't work?" That's a sobering thought. But how many times have you seen a speaker fumble around and lose credibility because he had no backup plan when his PowerPoint presentation decided to take a personal day?

Here are some backup plan ideas:

1. Bring a backup copy of your PowerPoint presentation on a flash drive.

2. Have at least one extra laptop with you, preloaded with the presentation.

3. Print out a set of your PowerPoint slides in the "Notes" layout (slide visual on top, notes on the bottom) and have it at the ready so that, if necessary, you can use it the way people used 3"x5" note cards for speeches back in the day.

4. Bring a clean copy of your handout in case you need to make a few last-minute copies for unexpected guests. (For more on what makes a good handout, see Chapter 16.)

5. When you're supplying some or all of the presentation equipment, be sure to pack an extension cord, an extra projector light bulb, and all the necessary cords for your laptop, projector, and so on. Even when the venue is providing all the equipment, I know plenty of speakers and companies who wisely bring their own, "just in case."

6. Arrive *at least* 30 minutes early at the venue for *any* speech. No blue chip client ever awarded additional business to the "sorry-we're-still-setting-up-because-the-traffic-was-crazy-today" team.

7. For out-of-town presentations, always make sure you wake up in the city in which you're presenting. Don't let delays or cancellations at DFW or JFK cost you the BIZ. Call me crazy, but I've found that even the best presentation falls flat when the presenter is not actually present.

8. In case your allotted speaking time is cut short, have shorter versions of your presentation ready to go. Determine ahead of time what you would cut out if your 60-minute talk is suddenly cut down to 30 minutes, 20 minutes, or even 10.

9. Discuss a specific backup plan with your team (if you have a team) *ahead of time.* Not in the elevator on the way up to the meeting. What will each person's role be if something goes wrong? What will you do if a key team member suddenly can't attend? Who will take the lead on technology issues?

During Your Speech: What to Do When Things Go Wrong

Despite having the best backup plan, things can happen that are beyond our control. Instead of letting a mishap derail your entire speech, why not harness the power of the situation and use it to your advantage? As Jimmy Dean, famous singer, actor, and sausage king, once said, "I can't change the direction of the wind, but I can adjust my sails." The polished presenter will "adjust her sails" when presentation mishaps occur by performing presentation triage.

Perform presentation triage.

First, ask yourself if the mistake is a big deal to your audience, or just to you. If you're the only one who notices it (e.g., a key slide is missing or you completely forgot to mention your best case study), don't waste precious time or presentation capital on it. Decide that it doesn't matter and move on.

However, if the audience clearly notices the gaffe or it seriously impacts the flow of your presentation, then the blunder has become the proverbial "elephant in the room" and the wisest course of action is to deal with it openly. Naturally, you want to acknowledge the hiccup in such a way that you:

1. Don't hurt your credibility,
2. Don't spend too much time on it, and
3. Enhance your relationship with the audience

Acknowledge it with an off-the-cuff remark...and a smile.

One approach is to trust yourself and be willing to say the first thing that comes to mind (as long as it's rated G). Whatever words escape your lips will be the most natural, authentic, and probably the most humorous thing you could say. The reason your first, natural thought is often funny is because it's likely to be the same thing that is on the audience's mind. Giving voice to it is what makes it funny. So smile and act as if it's no big deal. Your audience will take its cue from you. They're likely to smile or even laugh along with you, which will release some of the tension in the room and even add to your likeability.

For example, a few years ago I was facilitating a business development seminar for 40 financial planners and was writing key insights on a white board. As I was writing and talking, I noticed a few smiles and chuckles in the audience. I looked back at the white board and realized that I had spelled the word "million" with an "a" instead of an "o." I remarked, "I misspelled the word 'million,' didn't I?" (Pause.) I then said, "Man, I wish these markers came with spell check." They laughed. I corrected the word and we moved on.

A little self-deprecating humor will make you more authentic to your audience and you might even score some empathy votes. Don't worry; chances are you won't say anything offensive or inappropriate. The key is to acknowledge the miscue, address it, and quickly proceed with the rest of the presentation.

Use a rescue line.

That said, some folks just aren't comfortable taking the proverbial governor off their tongues. They feel more confident if they have an "ad-libbed" response or rescue line ready to go. A rescue line works best when it appears as though you just thought it up. And it needs to be something you would naturally say in that situation. In other words, it must be genuine. If the line is something someone else would say, your audience will spot it from a mile away and it may actually add distance between you and them.

How do you know if a particular rescue line will work for you? The answer is more art than science. Have a few lines ready to unveil, and after using one, observe the reaction you get. Keep tinkering until you get it right. Here are some examples to get your creative juices flowing:

When you forget where you are in the presentation or your mind goes blank:

- "At my age, the only thing I retain these days is water." —Carol Weisman (a woman with her AARP card and the best non-profit consultant on the planet)
- "First it's the hair, then it's the memory." —Me (In case you haven't looked at the back of the book, I'm follicly-challenged.)
- "Does anyone know where I was headed with this?"

When the projector doesn't work, the light bulb burns out, or you have some other technical issue:

- "Can everyone see the black screen okay?"
- "Everything worked so well in rehearsal."
- "It wouldn't be a presentation without at least one technical glitch."
- "We're experiencing technical difficulties. Is there a 5th grader in the house?"

When you say the wrong thing:

- "I'm going to pretend that didn't happen."
- "Did I say that out loud?"
- "I guess it's time to replace my mental filter."

When something isn't funny that was supposed to be:

- "That seemed *a lot* funnier last night at two in the morning."
- "Some of these I do just for myself."

- "That is an example of time-lapse humor. You'll probably laugh about it on the way home."
- Allow a brief silent pause where you had hoped the audience would laugh, and then say, "...or not."

Be "In the Moment" So You Can Be Ready *for* Your Moment:
When Unexpected Opportunities Arise

Okay, you've got your backup plan and have arrived at your presentation venue at least 30 minutes ahead of time. In addition to being on time, arriving early will give you time to get energized for a great speech (see Chapter 25 on psyching yourself up), and to assess the presentation room and the mood of your audience. It will also help you tap into what is occurring at the venue right before your speech.

Even if you're tempted to go over your notes right before presenting, don't do it. Cramming doesn't work. And if you're lost in your notes, you might miss out on the opportunity to play off of what's happening in the room.

A client of mine was once giving a speech to a state business association. Aflac®, one of the sponsors of the meeting, was given an opportunity to address the audience just prior to his program. An Aflac representative stood up, made a few nice points about her company, and then threw stuffed animal ducks (the Aflac mascot) to people in the audience. She was engaging and fun, and the audience was eating it up. My client wanted to build on their enthusiasm and tap into the "animal vibe," so he scrapped his planned opening and instead began by telling the audience about a British research study he'd recently come across. The scientific study was designed to ascertain what people felt was the funniest animal in the world. True story. To identify the funniest, researchers crafted a joke that involved an animal. They then substituted a different type of animal into the joke each time it was told, and the resulting level of audience laughter was measured. The animal that elicited the most laughter would be considered the funniest in the world. The winner was…(you guessed it)…the duck, which narrowly beat out the monkey, the chicken, and the weasel. To top it off, he mentioned that the research project was, of course, sponsored by Aflac.

When my client said this, the crowd whooped and hollered. If he had been lost in his notes or too self-focused about his speech, he would have missed a golden opportunity to connect with the audience. Using a bit of information he had collected in his "Cool Things" file (see Chapters 12 and 13 on stories and other presentation enhancers), he was able to tap into the energy already in the room.

These moments of opportunity don't always present themselves. But you never know when they will. The key is coming to the presentation room early and so prepared and comfortable with your material that you can be "in the moment" and make adjustments on the fly.

Remember…

Regardless of what happens during your speech, your audience will take its cue from you. If they perceive that you're uncomfortable, they will become uncomfortable, too. But if they see you take a mishap in stride, they'll be happy to do the same. So, do your best to roll with the punches (figuratively), be ready to respond in the moment, and use life's surprises to your advantage.

FAST APP

Start two lists (on your smartphone, in your pocket notebook, or wherever works best for you):

The first will become your pre-presentation checklist. Think about every aspect of your next presentation: PowerPoint slides, your speech outline and notes, equipment, transportation, team member roles, etc. What contingencies do you need to plan for? Make a list that you can refine and go over before each new speech. This will be a powerful tool to add to your speaking arsenal.

The second will be a little more light-hearted. Start a running list of responses you use as minor hiccups occur in your presentations or your everyday life. Write down the first thing you say, especially if it's endearing or funny. Note what feels natural to you and generates a positive response from those around you. Consider incorporating one of these responses the next time something goes awry in your presentation.

Aflac is a registered trademark of Aflac Incorporated.

25

Psyching Yourself Up
Moments Before Your Talk

*The thing with pretending you're in a good mood is
that sometimes you can.*
—Charles de Lint
Celtic folk musician and storyteller

"I'm just not feeling it." Have you ever thought this to
yourself before facing a difficult challenge or unpleasant task? I
sure have. The truth is, we sometimes feel this way before
giving certain presentations as well. Whether it's the topic
(boring or difficult), the audience (antagonistic or indifferent),
or the time of day (right after lunch or at the end of the day)
that presents a challenge—or maybe you're just having the
proverbial "bad day"—some speeches may be hard to get
excited about. So, how do you get yourself in the right frame of
mind to deliver the best possible speech? There are several
strategies you can use to psych yourself up to perform more
confidently and effectively.

"Power Prime"
Professor Adam Galinsky at Columbia Business School looked
at the positive impact that changing one's mindset can have in
high stress situations like job interviews [or presentations]. In

order to improve one's frame of mind in such a situation, he developed a technique called "power priming"[1]. Power priming involves recalling a time in your life in which you felt powerful, particularly one that was interpersonal in nature (e.g., recalling the day you persuaded the Board of Directors to adopt your idea works better than remembering the time you ran a personal best in a 5k).

Take five minutes to write down a brief account of that powerful moment. Galinsky's research demonstrated that the simple act of writing down such a memory will create a more confident and powerful mindset. Why does this work? Because doing so allows you to reacquaint yourself with the authentically confident portion of your personality. It's not about faking it. Rather, it allows you to harness the power of the real you.

And it's effective with others. According to Galinsky, "There is something about how power-primed people presented themselves that others picked up on. They expressed themselves with more confidence and more persuasiveness and that led them to get better outcomes."

Listen to Music, Lift Your Mood

Music has an amazing capacity to instantly alter a person's frame of mind, so why not make it an ally? Recent research from the University of Missouri[2] found that participants successfully and consistently improved their moods by listening to upbeat music. (Note that the type of music matters, as listening to somber music had no such effect.) A key factor in this study was that the participants *wanted* to improve their states of mind. —They weren't indifferent to the process. Therefore, the next time you're asked to give a presentation that you're not particularly excited about, pair a few upbeat songs with a willing spirit to lift your mood and energize your delivery.

Recall a Favorite Quote

Some speakers carry around inspirational quotations or Bible verses to help inspire them before they present. Here are some favorite "get in the mood" quotes used by friends who are professional speakers and trainers:

- Brendan Sullivan, creativity expert: "You miss 100% of the shots you don't take." (Wayne Gretzky)
- Claire Keeling, productivity maven: "Real artists ship." (Steve Jobs)
- Andy Masters, leadership and sales speaker: "The question isn't who's going to let you, it's who's going to stop you?" (Ayn Rand)
- Dixie Gillespie, dynamite coach and consultant: "Nothing is impossible, some things just take longer." (Richard Bach)
- Scott Ginsberg, the nametag guy: "I am the person who can do this."

Visualize Success

Don't let negative self-talk about how miserable the speaking experience feels become a self-fulfilling prophecy. Instead, imagine how the audience will react *when* (not *if*) you do a good job. Research published in *Psychology Today*[3] showed that regardless of whether weight lifters were actually lifting hundreds of pounds or simply imagining doing so, their brain patterns were almost identical. In other words, just thinking about the activity was practically the same as doing it. (Unfortunately, *thinking about* going to the gym won't net the same *physical* results as actually going to the gym.)

You can reap similar mental benefits before your next presentation. Visualize key audience members smiling and nodding in agreement with you Picture yourself confidently stepping away from the podium at the end, knowing that you nailed it. Get excited about how you'll feel at that moment.

Shake a Few Hands

Another way to get into the right frame of mind before you speak is to meet and greet as many audience members as possible, especially if you'll be speaking to a group for the first time. Seeing familiar faces in the audience will help you feel more confident and at ease while speaking. Plus, you never know what you might learn. During even brief conversations, people sometimes divulge helpful information that can affect how you deliver your message. Did the company just land a huge client? Has there been a layoff announced that you weren't aware of? Are additional decision makers now in the room? So, arrive early and shake as many audience members' hands as you can. But be sure to bring your Germ-X®, especially during cold and flu season.

Strike a Pose

Harvard Business School Associate Professor Amy J.C. Cuddy reports that holding yourself in a "power pose" for two minutes prior to a big presentation or important meeting leads to optimal hormone levels, an increased sense of power, and a higher tolerance for risk. Not too shabby.

Here's how to achieve those benefits. A few minutes before your presentation, stand next to a table or desk and lean over it on both hands. Or, sit down and lean back in a chair with your hands behind your head and your feet up on a table. Both are classic power moves (but probably not the kind of moves you'd want to make during a presentation). You need to hold either position for at least two minutes in order for this to work.

Cuddy's research[4] shows that holding an extended power pose elevates testosterone levels (the hormone linked to dominance and power) by 19% and lowers cortisol (the "stress hormone") by 25%. This is the perfect chemical combination for anyone lacking confidence or feeling overwhelmed. Even if you can't arrive early to your next presentation, strike one of these power poses in your office beforehand and feel your confidence soar.

Just not feeling it? The only thing standing between you and a great state of mind going into your next talk is a few minutes spent using one of these mood-elevating techniques.

FAST APP

As you prepare for your next presentation, set an appointment on your calendar for 10 minutes before your talk. Literally block it off. And then be disciplined about selecting one of the six ways listed in this chapter to get yourself psyched up:

1. *Jot down a time when you felt powerful.*
2. *Listen to upbeat music.*
3. *Reflect on an inspirational quote.*
4. *Visualize success.*
5. *Arrive early and shake a few hands.*
6. *Strike a power pose.*

Note that variety is the key to keeping things fresh and maintaining the efficacy of these techniques. So take care not to use the same one over and over.

Germ-X is a registered trademark of Vi-Jon, Inc.

26

En Garde!
17 Weapons to Combat
Presentation Nerves

*If you're not just a little bit nervous before a match,
you probably don't have the expectations of yourself
that you should have.*

—Hale Irwin
3-time US Open golf champion

Picture this scene: You're just minutes away from delivering a speech. You've prepared admirably, you have your backup notes, and your visual aids are ready to go. There's just one problem: YOU'RE GRIPPED BY AN INESCAPABLE FEAR THAT SHAKES YOU TO YOUR VERY CORE. (Or, perhaps you're still feeling the effects of last night's double-queso chimichanga.)

Don't think this is something that only happens to you. Everybody gets nervous before speaking in public. And it's not just the common folk either. Many a celebrity, who you would think would have all the confidence in the world because he or she has built-in adoring fans, struggles with stage fright. There are U2's Bono, actress Scarlett Johansson, and the hard-to-define Lady Gaga, to name just a few.

So let yourself off the hook and recognize that nervousness is just a part of the process.

If nerves and jitters are going to be there, the question becomes: What are you going to do about it? I wish there were a quick and easy way to overcome nervousness when speaking in front of a group, but there just isn't. However, there are scores of little steps you can take to calm your nerves and deliver your presentation with more confidence.

Here is a list of 17 strategies, divided into three sections, to get the ball rolling. I'm not suggesting you use all 17 before every speech. Who has the time? Experiment with them, find the ones that work best for you, and then make those a part of your routine.

Things to Do
Well in Advance of Your Presentation

1. *Know your stuff.*

   This may not sound sexy, but it's true. Nothing goes further towards soothing your public speaking nerves than knowing exactly what you want to say and how you want to say it. Tim Russert was highly effective as moderator of *Meet the Press* because he out-prepared everyone else on the show (especially his guests). Deep familiarity with your content also helps the Q&A session go much more smoothly.

2. *Practice out loud.*

   If you are able to do a practice run-through of your presentation out loud at least one time before the actual meeting, your comfort and confidence will soar when you do it for a second time "live." Mouthing the words silently in your mind does not count. You can practice your speech out loud anytime, anywhere: in the shower, during your commute, or standing before your beloved pet. The time is there; finding it may require some creativity. If you're seriously pressed for time, rehearse these three key elements: your opening, your closing, and your transitions. That way you start strong, finish strong, and sound great when going from one topic to the next. (For more on rehearsing, see Chapter 23.)

3. *Remind yourself that it's not that big a deal.*
   Because it really isn't. Time for a little perspective here. Certainly, every presentation is important. You may even have a lot at stake, and it might feel like the entire world hangs in the balance. But please remind yourself that it is just a speech. Even if something goes wrong, you will live to fight another day. And remember, no matter what happens during your presentation, no one is going to die because of it. (Sorry, doctors, this does not necessarily apply to live surgical presentations.)

4. *Picture your audience ahead of time.*
   As you write your presentation, envision the people you'll be presenting to—what they're wearing, where they're sitting, the expressions on their faces, the concerns on their minds, what they need from your presentation, etc. Humanizing your audience makes them less ominous and more approachable.

5. *Visit the presentation venue ahead of time.*
   One of the best ways to calm your nerves is to visit the room in which you're going to speak ahead of time. This is

especially true if you're presenting in a venue for the first time. Stand where you'll be standing when you give the speech and imagine the audience sitting in front of you. Get a feel for the lighting, the layout of the dais or stage, where you'll place your laptop if you're using PowerPoint, and so on. Many trial attorneys visit courtrooms before the trial to get the lay of the land and to see a particular judge in action. This will go a long way towards reinforcing the feeling that "I can do this."

Things to Do
On the Day of Your Presentation

6. *Watch what you eat.*

The day of your presentation, try to eat foods that contain high amounts of tryptophan, an amino acid that reduces anxiety (but not too much; you don't want to fall asleep). Some foods that fall into this category are turkey, nuts, cheese, and flax seeds.

Also, avoid caffeinated beverages. They can make you feel jittery. Instead, channel the natural adrenaline rush that commonly occurs when standing in front of an audience towards presenting with energy. If nature's willing to give you a hand, grab hold of it.

7. *Drink some OJ.*

You may have heard: Orange juice is not just for breakfast anymore. The vitamin C in OJ has been shown to lower stress hormones in less than 15 minutes. It will keep you hydrated in a fairly healthy way and its sugar will give you energy. A small amount is all you need (to minimize both restroom breaks and your calorie count).

8. *Plug into iTunes.*

Dr. Zbigniew Kucharski at the Medical Academy of Warsaw found that one of the best and fastest ways to deal with nervousness is through music. Dr. Kucharski observed that nervous dental patients experienced a five-fold decrease in negative feelings when they listened to relaxing acoustic music for 30 minutes prior to a dental procedure[1].

Now, you may not have the luxury of chilling out to your favorite tunes for half an hour prior to your speech, but even a song or two can go a long way towards soothing your nerves. Try to steal away to the nearest restroom or an empty hallway for a few moments prior to your speech. Then, pop in your earbuds, queue up a couple of favorite relaxing songs on your smartphone or iPod®, and let the music take the tension away.

9. *Make a fist.*

Right before you get up to speak, clench both fists as tightly as you can, hold for 10 seconds, release your fists, and then rest for 10 seconds. Repeat two times. This exercise only takes a minute, yet it effectively releases muscle tension and thereby helps you relax. (Caveat: Don't hold your fists up in the air like the Notre Dame Leprechaun. You don't want people to think you're looking for a fight. Simply clench your fists with your hands on your lap or naturally at your side.)

10. *Do a breathing exercise.*

You may not notice, but when you're stressed, you're more likely to take shorter, shallower breaths. This can actually add to your feelings of discomfort by increasing your nervousness and clouding your concentration. Take time to slow your mind and body down by practicing deep, diaphragmatic breathing. This will increase your circulation, loosen your muscles, and lessen stress.

Here's how to do it: Breathe in deeply through your nose, drawing in as much air as possible and allowing your stomach to rise. This will force your diaphragm—the muscle located under your ribs and above your stomach—to expand. Then, exhale through your mouth slowly and evenly, allowing your stomach to fall and pushing out the tension. Breathe slowly, deeply, and evenly like this a few more times. Consider adding a positive mantra (e.g., "I am sooo relaxed.") as you do so. It may take a little practice to find a rhythm that works for you, but when you do, you may be surprised at how much tension this relieves and how relaxed you become.

Things To Do
During Your Presentation

11. *Move around.*

Get out of the self-imposed phone booth. While you're speaking, be sure to use the full "canvas" of the room or stage. Moving your legs and arms naturally (as opposed to statue-like stillness) is a terrific way to expel nervous energy.

A couple of suggestions: Take two to three steps in one direction, plant your feet, and make a point. Repeat as needed. Similarly, try to make gestures out on either side of your torso to get blood flowing and your muscles in motion. Simply put, your nervous energy has to have an outlet and physical movement releases that energy in a good way. (The other option is uncontrolled shaking and twitching. Your choice.) (For more on movement and gestures, see Chapter 18.)

12. *Practice Eye-to-Eye Contact.*

If you stress out at the prospect of speaking in front of a large group of people, then don't speak to large groups. What? Instead, deliver your speech point-by-point to one person at a time in your audience.

Here's how it works: First, lock eyes with one person and deliver a complete thought to him or her. Then, pause briefly in silence while you look for the next person to talk to. Lock eyes with that person and repeat the process. This technique works no matter how large your audience is. As an added bonus, you'll be able to read your audience more clearly and come across as trustworthy and poised at the same time. (For more on Eye-to-Eye Contact, see Chapter 17.)

13. *Smile.*

Even if you would rather jab a fork in your eye than make a presentation, you can feel less stressed *and* project confidence by doing one simple thing: smiling. The benefits are numerous.

First, scientists have known for years that smiling makes a person appear more confident and approachable. They've also found that smiling is infectious. This means that when you smile at your audience (despite the nervousness you may be feeling), they will likely smile back at you. And when you receive this positive "social feedback," your own mood will be elevated.

But there's more: As reported in *Psychology Today*[2], the physical act of smiling provides your brain with neural or "facial feedback" as well. This means that when you smile, your brain senses the flexion of certain facial muscles. It interprets this as, "Oh, I must be happy," and produces endorphins ("happy hormones"). These, in turn, cause you to smile more, reducing your anxiety, and lowering your blood pressure and heart rate.

Finally, recent research published by the National Institutes of Health[3] finds that a smile has another effect that is especially good for speakers: They discovered that people who smile are perceived to be more intelligent than non-smilers.

So, even if you don't feel like it at first, when nerves start to overtake your next presentation, do as the old standard says and "Put on a Happy Face."

14. *Pause for Power.*

Believe it or not, as a speaker, you do not have to fill every single nanosecond of your time with words or some kind of vocal utterance. For whatever reason, most speakers are uncomfortable with silence. Please give yourself permission to pause from time to time. When you pause for a few seconds, it combats nervousness by giving you a chance to catch your breath, get centered, remember what you want to say next, and modulate your pace. On top of all that, your audience will perceive a purposeful pause as a nice respite from hearing you talk, giving them a chance to process what you just said while looking forward to what you will say next. (Read more about the power of a good pause in Chapter 19.)

15. *Remember that the audience can't tell how nervous you are.*

The number one comment I hear from participants in my workshops after they see themselves on video giving a speech is that they don't appear nearly as nervous as they thought they would, given how they'd felt internally. There are two important truths to note here.

First, your audience will assume the best of you—that you're in control, feeling good, and are ready to give a fine presentation—because it's in their best interests to do so. They want you to be a good speaker for their own benefit. Who sits down to listen to a presentation with the hope that the presenter is dreadful? Nobody. So, unless you tell them how nervous you feel (don't) or you shake hysterically (you won't), you begin with the benefit of the doubt.

Second, just as my workshop participants have witnessed about themselves, one's nervousness on the inside is not often readily apparent on the outside.

A nervous presenter should take great comfort in these truths about his audience.

16. *Don't read too much into audience body language.*

One of the things that makes speakers nervous (unnecessarily) is how they perceive the body language of their audience. We all love positive feedback, and it's certainly important to gauge the pulse of the crowd, but not everything that happens in the audience is a direct result of something the speaker does.

For instance, there's a persistent body language myth that when people cross their arms across their chest, it means they are "closed off" to what they're hearing and subtly sending a negative message about it. This is not necessarily the case. According to Joe Navarro, former FBI Counterintelligence Agent and author of *What Every Body is Saying*[4], crossed arms in front of the chest can mean up to nine different things, and *none* of them is a signal of resistance to an idea or person. Navarro contends that crossed arms, among other things, are more likely a "self hug" (meant to make the person feel soothed and more comfortable), a way to mask anxiety or fear, a power pose (think bouncers at a bar), or even just a sign that the person is feeling cold and trying to stay warm.

So the next time you spy someone crossing his arms while you're speaking, remember: It likely has nothing to do with you. Similarly, if someone stands up to leave in the middle of your presentation, it's more likely she had to address an urgent matter than that your speech wasn't worth staying for. And if an audience member has a grimaced expression on his face, he might be thinking about a sick loved one at home (or a thousand other things unrelated to you).

Certainly be attentive to your audience and their demeanor. If large-scale numbers are "tuning out," see Part Two of this book ("Making it Engaging"). And if you want to ensure you're well energized before your next speech, see Chapter 25 on psyching yourself up. Otherwise, remember: If you prepared well and are delivering solid information in an engaging manner, *you're fine*. Don't let the audience's body language dictate your level of confidence. Because you might just be reading them incorrectly.

17. *Do it more often.*

Psychologists have known for years that the more you confront your fears by doing the things that scare you (assuming they're not actually dangerous), the less intimidating they become. As Dr. Noam Shpancer explains in *Psychology Today*[5], this is based on the nervous system mechanism called "habituation." In simple terms, the more familiar something becomes, the less it causes us to feel anxiety. That's why psychologists often use "exposure therapy" to help their patients who suffer from anxiety. By repeatedly allowing themselves to be exposed to their fear, over time the patient becomes "habituated" to (or gets used to) the fearful situation, and its power to elicit anxiety in them becomes lessened (particularly as they see that no harm befalls them in the scary situation).

A corollary to this is that avoiding anxiety-producing situations tends to cause the fear of them to grow. This is because avoidance prevents habituation. Not only that, but as Dr. Shpancer explains, avoidance can lead to feelings of failure and weakness, and cause the sufferer to miss valuable confidence-building opportunities for practice and mastery.

Here's the good news: Exposure therapy is an incredibly powerful tool. Confronting your fears is not only a physiological antidote to anxiety. It also brings about a sense of accomplishment and empowerment and helps you develop skills and mastery, which, in turn, reduce the need to worry.

The single most powerful way to address public speaking-induced nervousness is to do it more often. So, conduct a little "exposure therapy" for yourself: Look for little opportunities outside your professional life to get up and speak in front of people, even (or perhaps especially) if it's only for a few minutes. Make a toast at your brother-in-law's 50th birthday party. Stand up to share your thoughts at a neighborhood association meeting. Give a volunteer committee report at your child's school. The more often you take on these small challenges, the more you will grow in confidence and reduce your fear of the big ones, and the easier and more enjoyable public speaking will become.

FAST APP

Select one strategy from each of the three sections above (Things to Do: Well in Advance of Your Presentation, On the Day of Your Presentation, and During Your Presentation). Then, try them out the next time you give a talk. If they work well, keep doing them and consider adding other strategies. If a particular strategy doesn't help you as much as you'd like, identify another one and give it a try. There isn't a one-size-fits-all solution, so keep experimenting until you find the tactic(s) that work best to keep your nerves under control.

---

iPod is a registered trademark of Apple Inc.

27

The Postmortem:
Your Improvement Accelerator

No matter what happens on the field or in life,
the most important play is always the next one.
—Andy Cavalier, high school football coach

It's a balmy August evening at the Helium Comedy Club in Philadelphia and comedian Dave Hopping has just finished a killer set in front of an enthusiastic crowd of fans. Dave and his comedy partner, Brian Smith, know their gig went well. But in the spirit of always trying to make the next one better, they've videotaped their entire performance for critiquing later that night.

Much to Dave's chagrin, as he watches the videotape, he notices that in the middle of the set, he starts scratching his back with his left hand. This is no ordinary scratch, mind you. It looks as if he's trying to remove an entire layer of skin. And he does it for minutes at a time. It's highly distracting, and he wonders how the audience managed to look past his feverish scratching to hear his jokes.

Armed with this newfound knowledge, Dave is on the lookout for this personal tic during his next performance. As a result, he is able to stop himself before he even starts it the next night. The result? Less distraction and even more laughs.

The same principle applies for performances of any type, including public speaking. The best way to develop your skills is to spend a few minutes after each presentation reviewing and analyzing it. I call this the speech "postmortem." (Yes, *I know* the term "postmortem" typically refers to an autopsy. And while Dave and Brian "killed" at the comedy club, I'm *pretty sure* no one—including you—has died from your presentation. So let's look at the "post" and not the "mortem.")

How to Evaluate Your Performance

There are three main ways to assess your performance. The best is a video or audio recording because of the inherent objectivity in the recording. As my high school football coach used to say about game film, "The big eye in the sky don't lie." The next best feedback is from an attentive colleague or friend. Last, but not least, you can analyze your own speech with the help of a pen and paper and just a few moments of quiet, objective reflection. Whichever method you use, the postmortem is the most effective way to identify and correct bad habits, and recognize and strengthen good ones, thereby improving your public speaking skills.

Here's a bit more about each of these methods. You may use just one or up to all three.

Tape Yourself: Video or Audio
Follow Dave Hopping's example and arrange to videotape your presentation. Alternatively, make an audio recording.
- Watch or listen to it that night before your head hits the pillow. If you have video, try watching it for a few minutes with the sound turned off to focus solely on your

movements, gestures, and overall body language. It may surprise you, but will certainly be enlightening. Then, watch it a second time with the sound on to zero in on the vocal aspects of your presentation.

- Make two lists. One list is your "keep doing" list, which should include things you did well and want to continue in future presentations. The second list is your "never again" list which, of course, is the list of things you want to eliminate from upcoming speeches.
- Look at each list prior to your next presentation.

Ask a Colleague for (Honest) Feedback

Ask a colleague or friend to observe your talk and arrange for her to provide five minutes' worth of feedback as soon as possible afterwards.

- Beforehand, give her one specific presentation skill you want to improve on so she can pay careful attention to that area—eye contact, stance, pace, etc.
- Afterwards, ask her to tell you what you did particularly well, and listen to what needs improvement. Allow her to provide you as much information as she observed or is willing to share.
- After the face-to-face with your "coach," take a few minutes to ask yourself, "Did I feel good about my presentation?" In other words, did your perception match the reality of what the audience (as represented by your colleague) saw?

Give Yourself a Report Card

As soon as possible after your presentation, carve out some time to assess your performance. First, give it an overall assessment. I like to assign my presentations a letter grade like back in school (A through F). Or, you may prefer to assess it on a 4-star basis like a movie review. Then, answer these kinds of questions:

- Was your speech clear and concise?
- Did you effectively deliver your Take-Home Message?
- Did you accomplish what you wanted to? If so, great. If not, what went wrong?
- Did the audience seem engaged? If not, where did you lose them? What could you have done differently to keep their attention?
- If the audience was given the opportunity, did they ask questions? What was the quality of their questions? Surface-y? In-depth?
- How was your physical delivery? Good Eye-to-Eye Contact? Natural gestures? How was your volume? Did your voice fill the room?
- Were you stuck standing inside the proverbial phone booth? Did you move around?
- Did anything go awry? —Was there an adverse reaction from the audience? Technical problems? Did your time get cut short? How did you handle it?
- Were you all set up and ready to go at least 15 minutes prior to the presentation? Or were you fiddling with the projector as people filed in? ("F7! Try F7!")

As with the other methods, answers to these questions will help you zero in on what you should continue to do as well as what you can do better next time.

Regardless of the method you choose, the postmortem is all about looking back before you go forward. Use an honest assessment of where you've been to chart a course for continuous improvement. Remind yourself of the strengths you want to continue. Then, focus on one or two things you want to improve upon for next time. Just remember: The postmortem only works if you refer back to it *prior to* your next presentation.

FAST APP

Beyond assessing the effectiveness of your physical delivery (which is extremely important), don't forget to critique the **content** of your presentation as well. Ask yourself these kinds of questions to be sure that the substance of the words you said were every bit as good as the way in which you said them:

1. Was my presentation well received?
2. Did I accomplish my goal?
3. Did people seem to get bored or confused at any point? If so, how could I have prevented that?
4. Were there any questions that caught me off guard?
5. How did I manage my time? Did I try to cover too much material in the time given?
6. At what point was the audience most attentive and engaged? How can I replicate and expand on this reaction in future presentations?
7. What one thing could I have done differently before my presentation that would have made me more successful during the presentation?
8. Am I satisfied with the amount of preparation I did? If not, how can I give myself a leg up for the next one?
9. What grade would I give myself on the quality of the content I presented?

Afterword

Great speakers are made, not born.

Perhaps the greatest thing about speaking in front of a group (scary as it may seem at times) is that anyone can become good at it. Seriously. It's unlike other endeavors, such as placing first in the New York City Marathon or winning *American Idol*, in which you either have the skills or you don't. (Not that those endeavors don't require practice; they do. But they also require some pretty hefty DNA.) Captivating an audience and speaking confidently in front of a group is open to anyone who wants to do it well. If you think about it, you've been communicating and influencing audiences ever since you learned to talk. Now it's just a matter of putting those skills and the principles in this book to good use.

All it takes is desire. Do you want to captivate your next audience? If you do, there's nothing preventing you from standing up in front of a group of people and owning the room. The best part is that, the more you do it, the more you'll begin to like it. (Okay, perhaps it'll never be your favorite thing, but you'll certainly enjoy it more.)

So go for it. Map out a plan. Craft a compelling message. Think about your visuals. And then practice. Practice, practice, practice. (Did I mention practice?) Do these things and you will be unstoppable. Not only will your career be enhanced, but your confidence will be bolstered as well. And most important: You'll feel amazing for having achieved something great.

Happy speaking!

Acknowledgments

This book would not have been possible without the contributions and support of the following people. My sincere thanks and heartfelt gratitude go:

To Mary Anne Hughes, my better half and the best thing to ever happen to me. She patiently listened to me for four-plus *years* as I wrestled with chapter titles, book structure, and which stories to include. Not only did she listen, but she also offered insight and editing help every step of the way.

To Carolyn Bond, my editor at Editorial Arts for her wisdom and direction in writing this book, for her admonishment to continually make the book better (even when I thought we were already "there"), and for her laser-like attention to detail. This book is immeasurably improved because of her input.

To Jack Hughes, my father and business mentor, who supported my decision to start my own speaking and training company, even though it meant leaving the family business.

To Bill Hughes, my brother, who encouraged me to pursue my dream of professional speaking while we were drinking coffee at Saint Louis Bread Company. His support was the final nudge I needed to step out of my comfort zone.

To Scott Ginsberg, Carol Weisman, and Andy Masters, my "mastermind group," who egged me on month after month with their constant refrain, "How's your book coming?"

To Southwest Airlines, the greatest airline on the planet. Most of this book was written at 33,000 feet jetting between speaking engagements in Chicago, Los Angeles, New York, and Houston. Thanks to Southwest's traveler-friendly change policy, generous Rapid Rewards program, and comfy leather seats, this book was a lot easier to write.

To Doug Bacon, Peter Sloan, and Jennifer Baskel, my early champions and supporters of *Hit Your Stride, LLC*. These remarkable people believed in me before my resume warranted it.

To the London Fishmongers, for their silent, nearly imperceptible support behind the scenes.

To Seth Godin, for inspiring me to ship.

Appendices

Appendix A: *Universal Speech Outline* Template

Appendix B: *Know Your Audience* Worksheet

Appendix C: How to Write a Speech in Five Minutes

Appendix D: Recommended Resources

Appendix A:
Universal Speech Outline
Template

Presentation Subject/Title:

BEGINNING
    SPARQ:
    Take-Home Message:

MIDDLE
    Rationale:
    Point #1:
    Point #2:
    Point #3:
    Additional Points? (if necessary)

END
    Q&A (questions you anticipate being asked):
    Call-to-Action:

Evaluation (Postmortem)
(after the speech is over, but on the same day)
    1. What I did well:
    2. What I want to improve upon:

Appendix B:
Know Your Audience Worksheet

To make sure your presentation resonates with them, you need to know your audience inside and out. Here are some good questions to ask as you put your presentation together.

WHO?
- Who are they? What's their background?
- What is the mix of my audience with regard to age, industry experience, seniority, gender, ethnicity, nationality?

_____

_____

_____

WHAT?
- What else is on their minds?
- What do they already know about the topic?
- What might prevent them from listening to and acting on my information?
- What motivates them? What keeps them up at night?
- What are their pre-conceived notions about me? My department? My organization? My profession?

_____

_____

_____

WHEN?
- At what time of day am I presenting? Morning? After lunch? End of the day? (Remember, the afternoon is often the most challenging and requires more audience interaction.)

_____

_____

WHERE?

- Where am I presenting? My office? Their office? A neutral site?
- How familiar am I with the surroundings?
- Do I know the Ins & Outs of the technology in the room?

_____

_____

WHY?

- In case the audience is wondering: Why am I the one giving this presentation?
- And why now?

_____

_____

_____

HOW?

- How does my audience like to process information?
- What am I going to do to engage all four learning styles (print, visual, auditory, kinesthetic)?

_____

_____

_____

Extra-Critical Step:

- What section or part of my presentation is most likely to elicit the most questions from or discomfort in my audience?

_____

_____

_____

- What am I going to do to overcome their resistance? How can I minimize the impact of the less palatable portions of my speech?

_____

_____

_____

Appendix C:
How to Write a Speech
in Five Minutes

If you're ever asked to give a presentation at the proverbial last minute, and only have five (real, not proverbial) minutes to prepare—which happens more than you might think—, here's an approach you can use to make the most of the situation.

One caveat: This five-minute approach works only if the presentation is on a topic with which you're intimately familiar. In other words, you can't expect to sound smart pontificating on a subject about which you know next to nothing. For this exercise, let's assume you're the subject matter expert.

While you won't have time to polish your speech or get it exactly right, by following these three steps, in order, you will come across as poised, at-the-ready, and intelligent.

1. Identify your Take-Home Message.
2. Gather a few supporting facts.
3. Determine a powerful conclusion.

Let's unpack each part.

1. ***Write down the Take-Home Message*** you want your audience to walk away with. What's the ***one thing*** you want your listeners to do, think, or feel based on your comments? Everything in your speech needs to work towards accomplishing this goal.

2. ***List every piece of supporting material*** you can think of that reinforces your Take-Home Message. These could be general observations or specific data points (if they're available). Write them down as bullet points. Don't worry about the words or grammar. Just get as much as possible of what's already in your brain down on paper in rapid-fire, non-judgmental, stream-of-consciousness style. Then, circle the two or three most important facts or data points and plan to use these in your speech.

I recommend starting with the above two steps so that, if you run out of time, at least you've scripted your main message and a few key supporting points. This alone will give you a good foundation for your talk, assuming you know the subject matter well. Then, if time allows...

3. ***Choose a powerful conclusion or Call-to-Action*** (CTA). What do you want to be at the top of your audience's minds as they file out of the room? Re-state your Take-Home Message in action-oriented terms so that your listeners know exactly what they're supposed to know or do. If you can complete this third step, it will help you finish especially strong.

Feel free to bring the piece of paper with your outline on it to the front of the room. —It should be all you need in the way of notes.

While your presentation probably won't be compared to MLK's "I Have a Dream" speech, it will get the job done.

Appendix D:
Recommended Resources

An open mind leaves a chance for someone
to drop a worthwhile thought in it.

—Anonymous

Books, Online Resources, and Organizations

For those of you inclined to dig a little deeper, here's a list of great resources to spur you on in your journey to becoming a captivating speaker.

Books

* *Conquer Your Speech Anxiety* by Karen Kangas
  This very practical book comes with both a workbook and CD as helpful resources.

* *Beyond Bullet Points* by Cliff Atkinson
  Atkinson shows how any presenter can create and deliver compelling PowerPoint slides without using any text-only bullet slides. He helped the plaintiff's lawyers craft the opening statement PowerPoint that resulted in the $253 million Vioxx judgment.

* *Presentation Zen* by Garr Reynolds
  Reynolds seamlessly applies the ideas of simplicity and beauty to presentation design. The results are astounding.

* *The Story Factor* by Annette Simons

If you want to learn how to tell a story in a variety of settings, *The Story Factor* is one of the best on the subject.

- *Good in a Room: How to Sell Yourself (and Your Ideas) and Win Over Any Audience* by Stephanie Palmer
  Palmer, a former MGM movie executive and veteran of 3,000 movie pitch meetings, offers terrific advice beyond traditional presentation skills. She also explores pre- and post-meeting dynamics.

- *Say It with Charts* by Gene Zalazny
  This former McKinsey consultant has written a very good book about the importance of matching up your data with the right chart format. He shows how selecting the correct chart for your information can spell the difference between success and failure.

Online Resources
- www.TED.com
  TED, as many know, stands for Technology, Entertainment, & Design. Its site features the world's best thinkers and leaders, each giving the "speech of their lives" in 18 minutes or less.

- www.slideshare.net
  Think of Slideshare as YouTube for PowerPoint presentations. You'll find thousands of slide presentations on just about every topic from business to personal pursuits to...you-name-it.

- www.prezi.com
  Prezi is an innovative presentation platform and a nice alternative to traditional PowerPoint slides. There are both free and premium versions available.

Organizations

- Toastmasters International
  (www.Toastmasters.org)
  Toastmasters is the premier organization for people who want to improve their presentation skills in a supportive atmosphere. There are 70,000 clubs in cities around the world that meet at all times of the day, including on weekends. There's sure to be a convenient meeting in your neck of the woods.

- Speaking Circles International
  (www.SpeakingCircles.com)
  Speaking Circles' purpose is to provide "relational presence training for those called to make a difference." While similar to Toastmasters, the key difference is that Speaking Circles focuses mainly on easing people's fear of public speaking.

- Pecha Kucha
  (www.pecha-kucha.org)
  Pecha Kucha (derived from the Japanese word for "chit chat") started in Tokyo in 2003. Essentially, it's a presentation format that calls for presenters to use just 20 slides (mainly pictures) that are shown on a screen for 20 seconds each and advanced automatically. Every presentation is, therefore, just 6 minutes and 40 seconds

long. As this book went to press, there were 922 cities hosting Pecha Kucha Nights, so you can probably find one in a city near you.

•   National Speakers Association
    (www.NSAspeaker.org)
    For those of you who are interested in becoming a paid professional speaker, NSA is the place to go. While it is tailored to meet the needs of the full-time professional speaker, local NSA chapters provide a great opportunity to meet and interact with speakers who are at the top of their game.

Resources at HitYourStride.com
This leading-edge site features tons of great resources, including videos, articles, and audio learning programs, such as:
Influence: The Art & Science of Changing Minds
Instant Access: Making Great & Lasting First Impressions
Leave 'Em Laughing: The Serious Impact of Humor
Telling Stories to Engage & Inspire

Customized Programs In-Person and Online
Steve has been wowing crowds and helping people become amazing communicators for over 20 years. If you and your team need a keynote address, innovative presentation skills training, help in becoming more influential, or a new take on business development, give Steve a call at 314-821-8700.

Notes

Chapter 1 – "They Can't Make Me Speak": The Memphis Story
[1]Ingraham, Christopher. "America's Top Fears: Public Speaking, Heights and Bugs." *Washington Post*. The Washington Post, 30 Oct. 2014. Web.
[2]Harvard Business Review. "Re: You can't manage without this." Message to Steve Hughes. 27 May 2010. E-mail.
[3]"Captivate." *Merriam Webster Online*. MerriamWebster, n.d. Web. 25 August 2015. Web.

Chapter 4 – Put Yourself in Their Shoes
[1]"Presentations That Appeal to All Your Listeners." *Harvard Management Communication Letter* 3 (15 June 2000): 4-5. Print.

Chapter 5 – Stick the Landing: The Call-to-Action
[1]Williams, Roy H. "How to Write Ads That Build Brands." *Entrepreneur*. Entrepreneur Media, Inc., 06 Feb. 2005. Web.

Chapter 6 – A Confused Mind Always Says "No"
[1]Iyengar, S. S., and Lepper, M.R. "When choice can be demotivating: Can one desire too much of a good thing?" Journal of Personality and Social Psychology. December 2000: 995-1006. Print.
[2]Iyengar, S. S., Huberman, G., and Jiang, W. "How much choice is too much?: Contributions to 401(k) retirement plans." Pension Research Council Working Paper. The Wharton School, University of Pennsylvania. October 2003: 6-11. Print.
[3]"Most Confusing High Tech Buzzwords of the Decade." *The Global Language Monitor*. The Global Language Monitor, 17 Mar. 2010. Web.

Chapter 10 – Great Visuals: Going Low-Tech for High Impact
[1]Peck, Nan. "Creating Slide Presentations." *Nan Peck.* Northern Virginia Community College, 31 Jan. 2013. Web.

Chapter 11 – Putting the Power Back into PowerPoint®
[1]Benefield, Justin and Cain, Christopher L. and Johnson, Ken H. "On Relationship Between Property Price, Time-on-Market, and Photo Depictions in a Multiple Listing Service." Journal of Real Estate Finance and Economics. Vol. 43, No. 3, 2011. Print.

Chapter 12 – Finding and Telling Good Stories
[1]Hsu, Jeremy. "The Secrets of Storytelling: Why We Love a Good Yarn." *Scientific American.* Scientific American, 18 Sept. 2008. Web.

Chapter 14 – Leave 'em Laughing: Adding (Appropriate) Humor
[1]Welsh, Jennifer. "Why Laughter May Be the Best Pain Medicine." *Scientific American.* Scientific American, 14 Sept. 2011. Web.
[2]Dunbar, R.I.M. "Social Laughter Is Associated with an Elevated Threshold for Pain." *Royal Society Publishing.* The Royal Society, 26 Aug. 2011. Web.
[3]St. John, Warren. "Seriously, The Joke Is Dead." *The New York Times.* The New York Times, 21 May 2005. Web.

Chapter 17 – The #1 Trust-Builder: Eye-to-Eye Contact
[1]Burgoon, J.K. and Coker, D.A. and Coker, R.A. "Communicative Effects of Gaze Behavior: A Test of Two Contrasting Explanations." Human Communications Research. 12, no. 4, 1986: 495-524. Print.

Chapter 20 – Managing Today's Shrinking Attention Span
[1] Lawson, Karen. The Trainer's Pocketbook. San Francisco: Wiley, 2009. Print.

Chapter 21 – Give 'Em the Gift of Time

[1]Perlow, Leslie. "The Time Famine: Toward a Sociology of Work Time." <u>Administrative Science Quarterly</u>. 1999. 44 (1), 57–81. Print.

[2]Locker, Melissa. "Survey: Americans Would Pay $2,700 For An Extra Hour a Day." *Time*. Time, 30 Oct. 2014. Web.

Chapter 25 – Psyching Yourself Up Moments Before Your Talk

[1]Galinsky, Adam. "Power Rewards." *Columbia Business School*. Columbia Business School, 13 May 2013. Web.

[2]Wall, Timothy. "Trying to Be Happier Works When Listening to Upbeat Music, According to MU Research." *MU News Bureau*. University of Missouri, 14 May 2013. Web.

[3]LeVan, AJ. "Seeing Is Believing: The Power of Visualization." *Psychology Today*. Psychology Today, 3 Dec. 2009. Web.

[4]Hanna, Julia. "Power Posing: Fake It Until You Make It." *HBS Working Knowledge*. Harvard Business School, 20 Sept. 2010. Web.

Chapter 26 – *En Garde!* 17 Weapons to Combat Presentation Nerves

[1]Kucharski, Dr. Zbigniew. "Musica Medica viratory-therapy applications for fear management in dental practice." *Nowa Stomatologia*. Nowa Stomatologia. February 2005. Web.

[2]Korb, Alex, Ph.D. "Smile: A Powerful Tool." *Psychology Today*. Psychology Today, 1 Aug. 2012. Web.

[3]Ingraham, Christopher. "Want People to Think You're Smarter? Smile More." *Washington Post*. The Washington Post, 7 Apr. 2014. Web.

[4]Navarro, Joe. "9 Truths Exposing a Myth About Body Language." *Psychology Today*. Psychology Today, 6 Oct. 20144. Web.

[5]Shpancer, Noam, Ph.D. "Overcoming Fear: The Only Way Out Is Through." *Psychology Today*. Psychology Today, 20 Sept. 2010. Web.

Index

About the Author

Steve is a handsome young man.
—Joan Hughes (Steve's Mom)

Steve Hughes, CSP[*], is president of *Hit Your Stride, LLC*, an international communications consultancy that helps people look and sound smart when they talk. A highly sought-after professional speaker and author, he is called upon by Fortune 500 companies, national associations, top law firms, leading universities, and non-profit organizations to electrify audiences and inspire more effective communication.

Prior to founding *Hit Your Stride* in 2005, Steve spent 14 years in the advertising business and was a partner in a 50-person ad agency where he made hundreds of presentations with millions of dollars on the line.

His work has been featured in *The Wall Street Journal* and *Businessweek* and on *NPR* and *BBC World News*. He is also the proud creator of "International Be Kind to Lawyers Day" (www.BeKindToLawyers.com), which is celebrated annually on the second Tuesday in April.

Steve holds a BA in French Literature and European History from the University of Kansas and an MBA in Marketing from Washington University's Olin School of Business, where he was awarded the prestigious Olin Cup.

He resides in St. Louis with his wife and their two well-behaved daughters.

[*] Certified Speaking Professional, a registered trademark of the National Speakers Association. The CSP is the highest earned designation from NSA and is held by less than 12% of speakers worldwide.

Steve Hughes wants you to captivate audiences.
For more info, please contact him at:
steve@HitYourStride.com
314-821-8700
www.HitYourStride.com

Made in the USA
San Bernardino, CA
18 June 2017